Acts
Living in the Power of the Holy Spirit

Bruce BICKEL
&
Stan JANTZ

HARVEST HOUSE PUBLISHERS

EUGENE, OREGON

Cover by Left Coast Design, Portland, Oregon

Cover photo by Steve Terrill Photography; www.terrillphoto.com

ACTS: LIVING IN THE POWER OF THE HOLY SPIRIT
Copyright © 2004 by Bruce Bickel and Stan Jantz
Published by Harvest House Publishers
Eugene, Oregon 97402
www.harvesthousepublishers.com

Library of Congress Cataloging-in-Publication Data

Bickel, Bruce, 1952–
    Acts: living in the power of the Holy Spirit / Bruce Bickel and Stan Jantz.
       p. cm. — (Christianity 101)
    ISBN 978-0-7369-0908-2 (pbk.)
  1. Bible. N.T. Acts—Commentaries. 2. Bible. N.T. Acts—Study and teaching.
I. Jantz, Stan, 1952– II. Title. III. Series.
    BS2625.53.B53 2004
    226.6' 07—dc22

                        2004003881

Contents

Part Six: Back to Jerusalem and On to Rome

A Note from the Authors

The book of Acts is one of the most interesting and instructive in all of Scripture. Acts is a history book that's full of action. It's always moving forward—from a Jewish church in Jerusalem led by Peter to a worldwide Gentile church led by Paul. Besides telling us about the history of the early church, Acts also gives us a thorough explanation of God's plan of salvation in Jesus Christ for all people everywhere. And it shows us how we can live as God's people and share God's plan by living in the power of the Holy Spirit.

Just a Little Help

We've taken a different approach from most commentaries and Bible studies in *Acts: Living in the Power of the Holy Spirit*. Lots of scholarly books will give you the technical theological concepts of the book of Acts. But if you simply want a little something to help you understand Acts and what it means to you personally, then this is the book for you. Each chapter is written to walk you though Acts step-by-step. We don't want to get in the way of your own personal study, but we do want to guide and encourage you.

Christianity 101™ Bible Studies

This Bible study on Acts is part of a series called Christianity 101 Bible Studies. We've designed this series to combine the biblical content of a commentary with the life applications of a Bible study. By reading this book and answering the questions, you will learn the basics of what you need to know so you will get more meaning from the Bible. Not only that, but you will be able to apply what the Bible says to your everyday Christian life.

And just in case you want even more help in your study of God's Word, we have listed some books that were helpful to us in our study of Acts. You'll find these at the end of the book in a section called "Dig Deeper." In addition, we have put together an online resource exclusively for users of the Christianity 101 Bible Studies. All you have to do is click on www.christianity101online.com (see page 174 for details).

How to Approach Acts

If you were to sit down and read Acts in one sitting (not a bad idea, by the way), you would notice that Acts falls into six parts. Each part traces the expansion of the church into a new geographic area and ends with a verse showing how successful the expansion was. In this book, we'll begin each of the six parts with an introduction telling you what is going to happen, and we'll conclude each part with the summary verse. We hope this will give you a better sense of the dynamic flow of this exciting book.

All that's left to do before you begin is to pray, and that just may be the most important part of your study. Ask God to guide you into His truth through the power of the Holy Spirit.

$\mathcal{A}$cts at a $\mathcal{G}$lance

Author: Luke, a Gentile and a physician. He's the only non-Jewish writer in the New Testament. Luke wrote Acts as a continuation of his Gospel.

Date: A.D. 62

Written to: Theophilus, who is also the recipient of the Gospel of Luke. Luke calls him "most honorable" (Luke 1:1), indicating that he is a man high up in the Roman government. Luke probably wrote Acts to show Theophilus that Christianity is good and Christians are good people. Beyond this single recipient, Acts is written for all Christians everywhere.

Purpose: Luke wrote Acts for several reasons: (1) to give an accurate account of the birth and growth of the Christian church, (2) to show that Christianity is for all people throughout the world, (3) to highlight the central message of the Christian faith, and (4) to show the Roman government that Christianity is commendable.

Themes: The Person of Christ, the baptism of the Holy Spirit, and the power of the church.

Sources: Since Luke was not one of the original 12 apostles, he was not an eyewitness of the life and ministry of Christ or the early days of the church. For the information in the first part of Acts, Luke probably relied on the records of local churches and personal interviews with eyewitnesses. Beginning in Acts 16:10, Luke is present in the story from time to time, so he had firsthand knowledge. When he wasn't there, he probably interviewed Paul.

$\mathcal{P}$art 1
The Church in Jerusalem
Acts 1:1–6:7

Once you start reading Acts, you won't take long to come to the key verse. It's Acts 1:8, the so-called "great commission," where Jesus tells His apostles to take His Good News message of salvation to the whole world. But before that happens, the church has to start.

In part 1 of Acts, we're going to witness the beginning of the church in the city of Jerusalem. All of the action is going to take place in this historic city. The Holy Spirit will come in power, thousands will turn to God by faith in Jesus, the believers will perform miracles, and Jewish leaders will begin to persecute the church. Hang on. You're in for an exciting ride!

Chapter 1

The Church Begins

Acts 1–2

*W*hat's *A*head

- Introduction and Themes (1:1-11)
- The New Twelve (1:12-26)
- The Holy Spirit Comes (2:1-13)
- The Church Is Born (2:14-47)

*C*hapter for chapter, verse for verse, word for word, the book of Acts packs more action and adventure than perhaps any other book in the Bible. You've got signs and wonders, shipwrecks and jailbreaks, dramatic conversions and powerful sermons. Structurally, Acts is first and foremost a book of history that traces the beginning and rapid development of the early church. Think of Acts as a bridge between the Gospels—those four biographies that tell the story of Jesus—and the letters (called *epistles*) written to first-century churches and individuals to provide instruction for faith and practice.

As Acts opens we see 120 believers huddled together in a second-story room in Jerusalem. By the end of the book—just 30 years later—these believers and others will take the Good News message of Jesus Christ from Jerusalem to every corner of the known world. How was this possible? What triggered the events and provided the catalyst for this incredible growth? What can we learn from this 2000-year-old history book that can help us today? What difference can the stories in the book of Acts make in your life? You're about to find out.

Introduction and Themes (1:1-11)

15⁶¹ Acts is sometimes referred to as "The Acts of the Apostles." The actions of the apostles, especially Peter and Paul, do play a crucial role in the events recorded in this book, but the first few verses of the first chapter bring out three other key themes.

Theme #1: The Person of Christ (1:1-3)

As you read Acts, keep in mind that this is the second volume of a two-volume set of books written by Luke about Jesus Christ. (Luke and Acts probably take up as many pages in your Bible as all of Paul's letters put together.) In volume one, Luke described the life and teachings of Jesus, culminating with His crucifixion and resurrection. In volume two, Luke begins by talking about the 40 days after Christ's crucifixion and ascension into heaven. Don't miss the incredible significance of these first few verses. Luke is focusing on the most important person—the living Christ, who was crucified, dead, and buried—and the most important event—the resurrection of Jesus—in the history of the world. Without Jesus and His resurrection, Christianity doesn't exist. No church, no salvation, and no hope—for any-body.

But Christ did rise from the dead, and He also made sure He provided plenty of hard evidence that He did. The Gospels record at least ten appearances of Jesus after His resurrection. Because of these "proofs," we don't have to wonder if Jesus is alive. We can know for sure!

$\mathcal{F}$aith and $\mathcal{P}$roof

Christianity is often called a "faith" because Christians must accept by faith that Jesus Christ is God's Son, sent to earth to save sinful humanity. At the same time, the Christian faith is based on rational proof, such as Luke writes about in Acts. As we will see time and again in Acts, faith alone in Christ alone—not mere knowledge about Christ—leads to salvation. But genuine faith will lead to proofs and reason as surely as it will lead to good works.

Theme #2: The Baptism of the Holy Spirit (1:4-5)

Just before Jesus experienced the passion of the crucifixion and the power of the resurrection, He called His disciples together in an upper room so He could give them some instructions. Among the many things Jesus told His disciples was some key information about the coming of the Holy Spirit. Here's what He said:

> *But when the Father sends the Counselor as my representative—and by the Counselor I mean the Holy Spirit—he will teach you everything and remind you of everything I myself have told you* (John 14:26).

Now, a few days after His resurrection, Jesus reminds His disciples what He said, only this time He refers to the baptism of the Holy Spirit: "John baptized with water, but in just a few days you will be baptized with the Holy Spirit" (Acts 1:5). As we will soon see, this will become the means through which the church is formed.

What Is the Baptism of the Holy Spirit?

The baptism of the Holy Spirit brings all believers together as part of the body of Christ (1 Corinthians 12:13). By His indwelling, the Holy Spirit becomes a part of the life of every believer, and by His baptism, all believers become a part of the body of Christ, otherwise known as the church. Even though we're going to see in Acts that the Holy Spirit occasionally comes to believers after a period of time, the Holy Spirit's indwelling and baptism usually take place immediately at the point of conversion.

Theme #3: The Power of the Church (1:6-11)

Besides the Holy Spirit, one of the main topics Jesus discussed with His disciples was the Kingdom of God. They aren't completely clear about it, so they ask Jesus when He is going to free Israel and restore the Kingdom. Jesus is quick to remind them, "The Father sets those dates." Those disciples were just as we are today. We want to know when Jesus is going to return to earth, and Jesus would say, "Look, don't try to figure out *when* I'm coming back in the future. Concentrate on *what* you need to do before I return. And here's what I want you to do":

*But when the Holy Spirit has come upon you,
you will receive power and will tell people about
me everywhere—in Jerusalem, throughout Judea,
in Samaria, and to the ends of the earth* (1:8).

This is the Great Commission, given by Jesus to His followers then and now. In order to fulfill Christ's commission, we need the Holy Spirit, who brings power to the church through His baptism. As William Barclay writes, "It is the whole lesson of Acts that the life of Jesus goes on *in His church*" through the Holy Spirit.

The New Twelve (1:12-26)

Put yourself in the sandals of the early believers. In the span of a few weeks, you have agonized over the public trial and cruel death of your Lord, rejoiced in His resurrection, and watched in bewilderment as your Master ascended into heaven after giving you His final instructions. Now it's time to get down to business, but there are only 120 of you—a pretty small number in light of the enormous task of reaching the world for Christ. Pretty daunting task, wouldn't you agree?

As you read Acts, you never get the impression that these Christ followers were ever discouraged. What's the key to this amazing attitude? It's pretty simple: "They all met continually for prayer" (1:14). You also notice that they didn't sit around waiting for things to happen. They got organized. They didn't mind that they only numbered 120. They worked together under the leadership of Peter, who gave a short speech addressing these two issues:

- *The replacement for Judas*—Judas was gone, so Peter suggested that "his position be given to someone else" (1:20). This was to make sure they were following the words of Jesus regarding 12 apostles sitting on 12 thrones, judging the 12 tribes of Israel (Luke 22:28-30).

- *The qualifications of an apostle*—Peter points out that the new twelfth man had to have the following qualifications:

   - He had to have been with Jesus.

   - He had to have witnessed the resurrection.

   Above all else, an apostle (someone who is *sent*) had to be a witness to the reality of Christ and the fact of His resurrection. Our faith is not based on hearsay or conjecture but on the objective truth of the risen Christ. This is the foundation of the church.

1562

The Holy Spirit Comes (2:1-13)

The next section describes the event promised by the Lord—the Holy Spirit coming to the believers in power. No doubt you've read this passage with its description of a "mighty windstorm" and "tongues of fire" and "speaking in other languages." What does it all mean? Were these signs and wonders unique to this Day of Pentecost, or do they still exist today?

- *The wind and fire*—Luke is specific when he says the coming of the Holy Spirit sounded like a mighty wind and looked like flaming tongues of fire. Wind is a symbol for the breath of God filling these believers in much the same way as God breathed into Adam His "breath of life" (Genesis 2:7), and God's breath gave life to the dry bones in

Ezekiel's vision (Ezekiel 37:5-6). Fire represents God's power and presence, as when God appeared to Moses in the burning bush (Exodus 3:2-5).

- *Speaking in other languages*—The Holy Spirit's coming during the Feast of Pentecost is no coincidence. Thousands of people from three continents jammed into Jerusalem speaking a variety of languages. When they hear the believers speaking their own languages, they are "bewildered." Whether the believers are actually speaking the languages or each person is hearing the message in his or her own language is unclear. What is clear is that this first instance of "speaking in tongues" serves a single purpose—to tell the world about Jesus and to fulfill the Old Testament prophecy pointing to the outpouring of God's Spirit.

What Is Pentecost?

Pentecost was an annual festival celebrated seven weeks after the day after Passover (Leviticus 23:15-16). That adds up to 50 days (the word *Pentecost* means "fiftieth"). All Jewish males were required to attend three festivals (also called *feasts*) in Jerusalem each year: Passover, Pentecost, and the Feast of Tabernacles. The Feast of Pentecost was originally the Feast of Firstfruits of the grain harvest, which has great spiritual significance. The 3000 who came to faith in Christ on this day (2:41) were the "firstfruits" of all who would follow.

The Holy Spirit: Beyond Baptism

The work of the Holy Spirit doesn't end when you become a Christian and He baptizes you into the body of

Christ. That just marks the beginning of what the Holy Spirit does in your life. As you grow in your faith, the Holy Spirit is your power for living. Jesus called the Holy Spirit a "Counselor" (John 14:16-17). The Greek word here is *paraclete,* which describes someone who comes alongside you as a companion to counsel, comfort, instruct, and advise you. As you live under the Holy Spirit's influence, He will do these things in your life:

- help you become more like Christ (2 Corinthians 3:18)

1656

- guide you into the truth of God's Word (John 16:13)

1550

- assist you in praying according to God's will (Romans 8:26)

1619

- give you one or more spiritual gifts (1 Corinthians 12:7) *The manifestation of the Spirit is given for the Common good*

1645

- empower you to be a witness for Christ (Acts 1:8)

1561

You also need to know that the Holy Spirit will do His work in your life when you let Him fill and control your life (Ephesians 5:18). When sin is in control of your life, the Holy Spirit is not (Galatians 5:16-17).

1680

1672

The Church Is Born (2:14-47)

1563

With the coming of the Holy Spirit—sent by God to remind believers about Christ, to baptize believers into His church, and to empower them to be His witnesses—the church was officially born. And what better way for this newborn body to grow than by proclaiming the Good News message of Christ. Here is the first Christian sermon ever preached, and it is delivered by Peter, the one Jesus called the Rock (Matthew 16:18).

1410

Peter's Sermon (2:14-36)

Space does not allow us to go into Peter's sermon in great detail. We would encourage you to read it carefully and watch for the following elements:

- *Salvation is for everyone.* Peter quotes from the Old Testament: "And anyone who calls on the name of the Lord will be saved" (Joel 2:32). Joel the prophet was looking forward to the Messiah, who would save Israel. Peter is making the bold claim that the Messiah is Jesus, and His salvation is for all people.

- *We are responsible for Christ's death.* Peter accuses his Jewish audience—and the lawless Gentiles—of Christ's death. In this sense all of us, Jews and Gentiles alike, put Jesus on the cross. Because He died for the sins of all people, Jesus' death also brings life to everyone.

- *God raised Jesus from the dead.* The resurrection is the final proof that Jesus is both Lord and Messiah. He's the one chosen and sent by God to save us from our sins and to make us right with God.

The People's Response (2:37-42)

The people are stunned by this powerful message. They ask, "Brothers, what should we do?" Peter lays out the simple Good News message of Christ, the same then as it is now:

1. *Turn from your sins.* In other words, repent. Turn your back on your sins and change the way you think.

2. *Turn to God.* Repenting is not enough. We must also turn to God, who will forgive our sins and save us because of Christ's death and resurrection.

3. *Be baptized in the name of Jesus for the forgiveness of your sins.* This kind of baptism is a sign that someone has repented and turned to God. Baptism doesn't result in forgiveness—it's the result of forgiveness.

4. *Receive the gift of the Holy Spirit.* The Holy Spirit is a gift from God given to all who believe.

The Believer's Joy (2:43-47)

What an incredible beginning to the church! On that Day of Pentecost more than 3000 people believed in Christ and were baptized by the Holy Spirit into the body of Christ. Luke lists ten characteristics of this new group of believers:

1. They were *learners.* That's what being a disciple means. These new believers were devoted to the teaching of the apostles.

2. They had *fellowship.* They met together regularly to strengthen and encourage one another.

3. They were people of *prayer.* This was central to their growth and development.

4. They were in *awe* of the Lord. There was a deep reverence for God and what He had done for them.

5. They witnessed *signs and wonders.* The missionary William Carey once said: "Expect great things

from God; attempt great things for God." That's the kind of people these early believers were.

6. They *shared* with one another. The early church was defined by people who took care of each other.

7. They *worshipped* the Lord together. King David wrote this about God's house: "A single day in your courts is better than a thousand anywhere else!" (Psalm 84:10). That's the way these believers felt about worship.

8. They were *joyful*. The joy of the Lord filled their lives.

9. They were *generous*. Nothing is worse than a stingy Christian. When we think about all God has done for us, we want to do things for others.

10. They had the *respect* of others. When we are living out our lives before God in the power of the Holy Spirit, people will notice and wonder what we have.

No wonder the church grew!

■ ■ ■

Study the Word

1. Why is Christianity useless without the resurrection
    of Christ? Would the teachings of Christianity be
    worth anything without the resurrection? Why or
    why not? (Before you answer, read what Paul said in
    1 Corinthians 15:17-19.)

*1649 No because we our sins would
not be forgiven*

2. Explain what this sentence means to you: "Genuine
    faith will lead to proofs and reasons as surely as it
    will lead to good works." What would your faith be
    like if you couldn't prove your beliefs? What kind of
    faith would you have if it didn't lead to good works
    (see James 2:17-18)?

1743 through faith comes good works

3. Christ told His apostles to tell people about Him in
    Jerusalem, Judea, Samaria, and the ends of the earth.
    What is your Jerusalem? Your Judea? Your Samaria?
    What can you do to take the message of Christ to the
    ends of the earth?

Wittness to strangers +

4. Only 120 people originally met together in Jerusalem (1:15). What can we learn from this small group of believers who would go on to change the world? Have you ever been a part of a small group that accomplished something great? What happened?

5. Read Ephesians 5:18. What does letting the Holy Spirit fill and control you mean? What are some practical things you can do to make sure this happens?

1680

Do not get drunk on wine, ✲
instead be filled with the
Spirit (read Bible - Pray)
✲ *which leads to debauchery*

6. The same Peter who became a champion for Christ once denied Him three times. What does that tell you about God and second chances?

There is always another
chance

7. Is repentance involved only in salvation, or must believers repent as well? How?

Chapter 2

Healing and Preaching

Acts 3:1–4:31

*W*hat's *A*head

- [ ] Peter Heals a Crippled Beggar (3:1-11)

- [ ] Another Great Sermon (3:12-26)

- [ ] Before the Council (4:1-22)

- [ ] The Believers Pray for Boldness (4:23-31)

*A*lthough signs and wonders were commonplace in the early church (2:43), only certain examples make it into Luke's history book. The miracle that takes place in Acts 3 isn't that unusual, but the events it triggers are extraordinary because they show how God's sovereign hand is at work to bring a great number of people into His Kingdom. The believers then recognize the significance of what God is doing. See if you can recognize it too.

Peter Heals a Crippled Beggar (3:1-11)

Luke doesn't tell us, but scholars speculate that as much as two years have passed since the Day of Pentecost.

Peter and John are on their way to worship at the Temple, showing that the apostles and other believers (who are all Jewish) continue to follow the Jewish traditions. As they are about to enter the Temple through the gate called Beautiful, a man lame from birth asks them for money.

Because giving money to beggars was considered noble in the culture, beggars often staked out the Temple gates, hoping for a legalistic handout. That the beggar asks Peter and John for money is no random happenstance. As we're going to see, God has a purpose in what is about to happen. Rather than give him money (which they don't have), Peter heals the crippled man "in the name of Jesus Christ of Nazareth." Instantly the man jumps up and begins to walk, leap, and praise God.

As you can imagine, everybody else going to the Temple to worship sees the miracle, and they aren't just impressed. Luke says they are "absolutely astounded!" As for Peter and John, they know exactly *what* is happening and *why* it happened. Jesus has given them the authority to do these things in order to "take this message of repentance to all the nations, beginning in Jerusalem" (Luke 24:47).

Can Miracles Save?

Miracles can heal and miracles can open people's hearts to receive the Word of God, but they can't save. The message of repentance must be preached and accepted by faith in order for people to be saved. Miracles still occur today because Jesus is still at work by His Spirit in the church, but true miracles of God don't occur in a vacuum. God always has a greater purpose in mind.

Another Great Sermon (3:12-26)

Now we see the reason for the healing. A huge crowd rushes out to Solomon's Colonnade, a popular meeting place in Jerusalem, to see firsthand what has happened. Picture Peter and John standing before the crowd with this former cripple standing beside them. Peter sees and seizes the opportunity to preach to the crowd. He delivers a sermon that contains many of the same elements of his sermon at Pentecost.

- *Jesus makes it all possible (3:12-13a).*
  Peter is quick to deflect the glory from himself and John. He explains that this miracle has been done in the name of Jesus Christ. Furthermore, God the Father—the God of Abraham, Isaac, and Jacob—has done this through His "servant" Jesus. The clear implication is that Jesus is the one who gives life.

- *You killed the author of life (3:13b-18).*
  Just as he did on the Day of Pentecost, Peter points the finger of blame at the crowd. They are the ones who killed Jesus, the author of life. Notice that Peter's tone toward the people of Israel is almost conciliatory. He concedes that they and their leaders acted "in ignorance." Furthermore, even the suffering of Christ was part of God's plan.

- *Turn from your sins and turn to God (3:19-26).*
  Here is the crux of the sermon. Peter calls on the listeners to turn from their sins and turn to God. This is what repentance means, and it's something every person needs to do in order to get right with God.

The Heart of Repentance

Wayne Grudem defines repentance as "a heartfelt sorrow for sin, a renouncing of sin, and a sincere commitment to forsake it and walk in obedience to Christ." All of us are born into sin. It was our sins—as much as the sins of those who actually killed Christ—that put Him on the cross. Jesus died for the sins of the world, but in order for His sacrifice to mean anything to us personally, we need to turn away from our life of sin in repentance, turn toward the one who forgives our sins, and accept Him by faith. Repentance + Faith = Conversion (2 Corinthians 7:9-10).

The Results of Repentance

When we repent, three things happen:

- Our sins are forgiven (3:19).

- Our parched lives are refreshed (3:20).

- Our future in Christ is secure (3:21).

Peter's Message in a Jewish Context

We can apply the principles of repentance to our own time and lives, but we also need to see Peter's call to repentance in the context of God's covenant to Abraham (Genesis 12:1-3). Christ the Messiah, a descendant of Abraham, came first to the people of Israel and then to "all the families on earth" (3:25). Richard Longenecker makes this comment:

> Here you have a member of the "righteous remnant" issuing prophetic denunciations

of Israel's part in the crucifixion of their Messiah and appealing to the people to turn to God in repentance for the remission of their sins.

Before the Council (4:1-22)

Peter finishes his sermon, and once again the Holy Spirit moves in the hearts of those who are listening. With the new conversions, the number of believers in Jerusalem has now reached 5000, and that's just the men! No wonder the religious leaders come join the party. Only they haven't come to celebrate. They're more like party crashers.

The Arrest (4:1-7)

Three groups come to see (and eventually arrest) Peter and John:

- *The leading priests*—These are the close relatives of the high priest, Caiaphas—the same one who condemned Jesus to death (Matthew 26:57-68).

- *The captain of the Temple guard*—This guy is second in command to the high priest.

- *The Sadducees*—These are members of a small but powerful Jewish religious sect who do not believe in the resurrection from the dead.

Most of those who arranged for the arrest and crucifixion of Jesus came from these three groups. They thought they had dealt with Jesus once and for all, and now they've got these pesky Christ followers to deal with.

*W*orth the *R*isk?

Peter and John were willing to preach even though they risked being arrested. In their case, the reward was well worth the risk. Thousands came to Christ that day, but you get the feeling that these fearless apostles, empowered by the Holy Spirit, would have preached if only one had repented that day. How about you? Is standing up for Christ in the public square—whether that's your workplace, your school, or your neighborhood—worth the risk? What's the downside? Ridicule? Embarrassment? Getting kicked out of the "in" crowd? Measure this against the reward of being used by the Holy Spirit to witness to someone who has no hope apart from Christ.

The Defense (4:8-14)

Peter and John are in front of a large group of power-ful religious leaders. They should be intimidated, but they are bold and articulate in their defense of the message Jesus has called them to preach. They are also clever! Notice how Peter turns the tables on these pompous officials. In effect he says, "Are you con-demning us for helping a poor crippled man?" Then he answers the question posed by the religious leaders, "By what power, or in what name, have you done this?"

Peter's answer is the Good News of Jesus Christ in a nutshell. He answers "clearly" so all can understand that the crippled man was healed "in the name and power of Jesus Christ from Nazareth, the man you crucified, but whom God raised from the dead" (do you think the Sad-ducees were squirming?). And Peter isn't finished. He brings in Scripture (Psalm 118:22), telling the council that Jesus is the cornerstone. In other words, He's the

Messiah—the only Messiah—sent to save those who are lost.

> *There is salvation in no one else! There is no other name in all of heaven for people to call on to save them* (Acts 4:12).

The Best Offense Is a Good Defense

In one of the two letters he would later write to the young church, Peter writes: "And if you are asked about your Christian hope, always be ready to explain it" (1 Peter 3:15). This is exactly what Peter did before the high council. He defended his position using three carefully calculated techniques. Learn from these:

1. He preached intelligently, using logic and reason.

2. He handled Scripture skillfully.

3. He was filled with the Holy Spirit.

The Warning (4:15-22)

Here's the result of Peter's masterful defense and witness: The accusers are dumbfounded. First of all, they are amazed at the boldness of these "ordinary" men who had no special training. How could they talk so intelligently and persuasively? The only conclusion the leaders can come to is that Peter and John "had been with Jesus." Second, they can't refute anything Peter said. The proof of the healing is the leaping beggar, so they can't deny that. All the priests and Sadducees can do is to stop them from ever speaking again. Of course, this is quite impossible, and Peter and John tell them so. "We cannot stop telling about the wonderful things we have seen and heard."

The Believers Pray for Boldness (4:23-31)

As soon as Peter and John are released, they go to the other believers and report everything that has happened. Notice the mind-set of these believers: They are united. Look at what they do: They pray. The content of their prayer (4:24-30) contains two powerful principles.

They Praise the Sovereign Lord (4:23-28)

During times of crisis, we have no greater comfort than the knowledge that God is sovereign. That means He is in control of the affairs of the world and our lives, even in tough times. "For the LORD is king!" wrote David. "He rules the nations" (Psalm 22:28). The believers know that the persecution they are experiencing is directly related to the persecution Christ endured.

> The church's willingness to keep spreading the Word despite the threats of peril is clear evidence that its message is truly from God.
>
> —*William J. Larkin Jr.*

They Pray for Boldness (4:29-30)

Notice that the believers don't pray for their persecution to be lifted. They don't pray that God would remove their obstacles. Instead, they pray for "boldness in their preaching." Their greatest concern is that the message of Christ's salvation goes out. Isn't this how we should pray? Too often we pray for our pressures to be eased, when instead we should be praying for strength and courage to overcome those things that stand in the way of our witness. We need to trust in Jesus, who said this to His disciples:

Here on earth you will have many trials and sorrows. But take heart, because I have overcome the world (John 16:33).

God's Exclamation Point (4:31)

Clearly God is pleased with the prayers of these precious believers. The building they are meeting in shakes, and they are filled with the Holy Spirit. Then they go out with the confidence they prayed for and preach God's message.

■ ■ ■

Study the Word

1. What purpose do miracles serve today? Why did the early church see more miracles than we see today?

2. The apostles' ministry was holistic—it included apologetics, healing, and preaching. Review Peter and John's approach to ministry in this chapter and how it included these elements. How can your church's ministry adopt this same philosophy of ministry?

3. Twice Luke has included the number of people who were saved as a result of the apostles' ministry (Acts 2:41; 4:4). What does this say about God's interest in "numbers"? What do you think is God's main

concern about the number of people who respond to His plan of salvation?

4. Have you ever been ridiculed for being a Christian? Have you ever been embarrassed? What did you learn from these experiences?

5. Read Acts 4:12. How would you explain this verse to someone who believes that Christianity is an "intolerant" religion? In what ways is Christianity intolerant? In what ways is it tolerant?

6. Must someone have formal Bible training (such as seminary) in order to be qualified to preach the Good News message of Christ? What is necessary? How do you think Peter was able to deliver such a knowledgeable and compelling message without any formal training? In what ways can you imitate Peter?

7. When should you get formal training in the Bible? What are the benefits of studying under others who have more experience and knowledge than you have?

Chapter 3

Body Life in Action

Acts 4:32–6:7

*W*hat's *A*head

*A*ny church with 5000 members these days is considered a "megachurch." Such a church probably has a beautiful campus with a large worship center, dozens of pastoral and administrative staff, and enough programs to keep you busy every day of the week. Even though the first-century church in Jerusalem had well over 5000 believers, nothing was "mega" about it—at least not in the external sense.

As we're going to see in this section of Acts, the church had no official campus or building, no paid staff, and no programming except for regular meetings in the public square around the Temple area, where the apostles would heal and teach the people. If anything was mega about the early church, it was the internal power of the Holy Spirit, who gave these believers boldness to preach God's message of life, regardless of the circumstances. At the same time, these believers did have some things in common with churches today. They had to care for and feed needy people. Oh, and there was also that little matter of discipline for people who were greedy. Once again, we can learn some great lessons as we do our best to serve Christ in obedience through the power of the Holy Spirit and His church.

Sharing Possessions (4:32-37)

You can tell from this passage that the Holy Spirit is at work in the lives of these believers. They are "of one heart and mind." This unity isn't superficial. They understand that they need to demonstrate their oneness in Christ and their witness to the world. This means they have to care for each other's needs. Economically, things in Palestine are bad because of political unrest and famine. Yet no believers suffer hardship.

They don't live together in a commune, and they still have their own possessions, but these believers don't look at them as private possessions. Instead, they share what they have with others. Truly this is a "powerful witness" (4:33) of the risen Lord, who said, "Your love for one another will prove to the world that you are my disciples" (John 13:35). No wonder "God's great favor was on them all."

Luke singles out the example of Barnabas, who later will accompany Paul. On his own, Barnabas sells a piece of property and gives the money to the apostles for those who are in need. As we will learn in the next section, neither Barnabas nor any of the other believers were obligated to do this. Their generosity came willingly from their hearts. Luke later describes Barnabas as "a good man, full of the Holy Spirit and strong in faith" (11:24).

Severe Consequences (5:1-16)

The church has already experienced opposition from the outside, and now comes the first instance of trouble on the inside. At first glance the punishment for what Ananias and Sapphira did may seem overly harsh (death is about as harsh as you can get), but in the overall scheme of things, it is completely appropriate. Watch how this series of events unfolds.

The Deception (5:1-4)

After the fine example of Barnabas, we see the contrasting story of Ananias and Sapphira, who hatch a plan to deceive the apostles. Perhaps they are caught up in the moment and want some recognition from the apostles and their fellow believers. Maybe they are just plain greedy. Whatever their motive, it isn't right. And to make matters worse, they try to pretend they are on the up and up, when in fact they are committing fraud against God. Not good.

Peter spots their ill-conceived plan from a mile away. He perceives that Satan—and not the Holy Spirit—has filled Ananias. The word *filled* in 5:3 is the same word used in Ephesians 5:18, where we are commanded to be filled with the Holy Spirit. It refers to control or influence. Ananias and Sapphira, who are believers, aren't possessed by Satan, but they have allowed themselves to be influenced by him. Peter pins down the issue: Ananias and Sapphira haven't lied to the apostles but to God. "Spiritual deception is heinous to God," writes Kent Hughes. "When we lie to believers, we're not lying to them but to the Lord."

The Father of Lies

This story teaches us two things about Satan. First, even though he was defeated by Jesus at the cross, he still "prowls around like a roaring lion, looking for some victim to devour" (1 Peter 5:8). Second, he is, as Jesus called him, "the father of lies" (John 8:44). We need to constantly be on guard against Satan's age-old schemes to influence us to lie to one another and to God. Deception is destructive to the church, and Satan knows it.

The Consequence (5:5-10)

Why do Ananias and Sapphira have to die? Their act of deception is judged severely because their dishonesty and their greed would have been destructive to the fledgling church. Lying is bad enough, but when believers lie to each other and to God, they destroy their testimony and make God look bad. (The opposite of this is giving God glory, which literally means "making God look good.")

The Holy Spirit Is God

Peter first says that Ananias has lied to the Holy Spirit (5:3), and then he says Ananias has lied to God (5:4). This clearly implies that the Holy Spirit is equal to God.

Romans 6:1

As believers, we should never think that we are exempt from God's judgment. If anything, God holds us more accountable than He does nonbelievers. Peter emphasizes this when he writes later, "For the time has come for judgment, and it must begin first among God's own children" (1 Peter 4:17).

Shock and Awe (5:11)

The judgment on Ananias and Sapphira is severe because it is an example. Evidently it works, because "great fear gripped the entire church." How about you? Do you see this story as ancient history for another time, or does it put a little fear in your own heart? Chuck Swindoll once said that to fear God is to take Him seriously and do what He says. God obviously hates deception, especially in His church. We need to pay attention to the deception in all of us.

Dealing with Deception

Kent Hughes offers this three-step method for dealing with our deception. First, we need to take an honest look at ourselves. Are we always truthful? Do we have a tendency to exaggerate or "embellish the truth"? Then, we need to come clean and lay the results before the Lord. Finally, we need to turn away (repent) from our sin and ask God to remove any habits of deception.

More and More Believe (5:12-16)

The same fear that grips the church also has an effect on people in the community (bad news travels fast). Still, many hear the Gospel, and more and more people believe. Why does this happen, especially when becoming a Christian in Jerusalem isn't exactly a popular choice (you have persecution on one hand and God's judgment on the other)? The church in Jerusalem demonstrates two reasons why people are attracted to Christ:

- They see the *power* of God at work dramatically changing lives.

- They see the *people* of God at work expressing generosity, honesty, and unity.

Opposition and Persecution (5:17-42)

The apostles have been teaching in defiance of the ban by the Jewish leaders. As you would expect, the high priest and his Sadducee friends react "with violent jealousy."

They arrest the apostles (apparently all 12 of them) and throw them in jail. In a scene that could go into an action movie, an angel springs the apostles and tells them to go back to the Temple to preach (this is the first of three jailbreaks recorded in Acts). The next morning the high priest and his officials convene the high council, also known as the Sanhedrin, a group of 70 officials.

Usually nothing is funny about opposition and persecution. But when you read this section, you can't help but see the humor. These 70 high officials are all dressed up and chomping at the bit to deal with these pesky apostles. So they ask their fancy Temple guards to fetch the offenders so they can begin their interrogation. Oops—they aren't there! The guards have been watching an empty cell. The leading priests are "perplexed" by all this, "wondering where it would end." Don't you love it? God has a way of confounding the wise.

When Power Is Threatened

What was true in the first-century church is true today: Those with vested interests in power and comfort—and with unbiblical views—will always see the truth of the Gospel as a threat. And even though they can't refute the truth, they will do everything they can to silence it.

The Priests and the Apostles Have Another "Discussion" (5:26-33)

As for the apostles, they are back at their favorite preaching spot, the Temple. The religious leaders find out and send the Keystone Kops (that would be the Temple guard) back to re-arrest them. The high priest is at his wit's end. He's so angry that he can't even say the name of Jesus. All he can come up with is, "Didn't we tell you never again to teach in this man's name?" (5:28). Peter and the apostles reply, "Of course we heard you. We're not deaf!" Actually, they didn't say that, but once again they tell the high priest and his council that they have to obey God rather than human authorities. And then they repeat the same three-point message as before:

- You killed Jesus.

- God raised Him back to life.

- Turn from your sins and turn to God for forgiveness.

This, of course, doesn't sit well with the council (they didn't like it the first time they heard it, and they don't like it now). So they decide to kill them all.

When Is Civil Disobedience Appropriate?

Scripture clearly teaches that we are to obey the government (Romans 13:1-7). Even Peter advises believers to "accept all authority" (1 Peter 2:13-17). So why are Peter and the apostles defying the authority of the Sanhedrin?

As Christians, we are not obligated to obey the government or any other authority when to do so is a sin. If the authorities prevent us from obeying God, as was the case with the apostles, then we need to appeal to the higher authority. According to Acts 5:32, the Holy Spirit is given by God to those who obey God. Conversely, our disobedience cuts us off from God.

An Unexpected Ally (5:34-39)

You should know two things about Gamaliel the Pharisee, who persuades the council to spare the apostles' lives:

- He was recognized as the greatest teacher of his day and was the spiritual father and teacher of Saul of Tarsus (Acts 22:3).

- He respected God's sovereignty, as evidenced by his statement: "But if it is of God, you will not be able to stop them" (5:39).

Gamaliel is no friend of the church (neither was Saul), but he does respect God. Let this be a lesson for us to not disregard the potential help of unbelievers. Just as

God used Gamaliel to help the apostles, He can use unbelievers (sometimes in high places) to help you carry out His will for you.

Rejoicing in Suffering (5:40-42)

The apostles' lives are spared, but their hides aren't. The council has them flogged with 39 lashes before releasing them. They could have gone home and licked their wounds, but that isn't even an option. Amazingly, they rejoice because "God had counted them worthy to suffer dishonor for the name of Jesus." And they make a beeline for—you guessed it—the Temple, where they continue to spread the message of Jesus Christ.

Getting Organized (6:1-7)

No church is perfect, not even the sometimes idealized early church. "Rumblings of discontent" arise because one group (the Greek-speaking Jews) feels that another group (the Hebrew-speaking Jews) are discriminating against their widows. So the apostles call a meeting and do some very instructive things:

- *They set their priorities.* The apostles know they need to focus on prayer and preaching, not administrating a food distribution program.

- *They delegated.* Rather than ignoring the issue, the apostles put qualified people "in charge of this business." The seven people they chose are wise, respected, and full of the Holy Spirit.

- *They commissioned.* The apostles don't treat "this business" lightly. They have a commissioning service where they pray for the seven-man committee and lay hands on them.

We need to learn from this process. Kent Hughes writes, "Delegation is at the heart of developing followers." It's also a way of developing future leaders. Stephen and Philip, two of the seven men chosen by the apostles, go on to become great leaders in the church. So the next time you are chosen to complete a task, don't complain—serve!

As the first section of Acts comes to an end, we see that the Jerusalem church is well established. The believers have carried out the first part of Christ's commission.

> *God's message was preached in ever-widening circles. The number of believers greatly increased in Jerusalem, and many of the Jewish priests were converted too* (Acts 6:7).

■ ■ ■

Study the Word

1. Is the account of the believers sharing possessions given by Luke as a command or an example? What happens to generosity when it becomes an obligation?

2. Explain the difference between these three words (use a dictionary if you want help):

   - communism

   - commune

   - community

   Which word best describes the church in Jerusalem? Why?   *Community*

3. Why was Barnabas an appropriate nickname for Joseph (4:36)? In what ways could you earn a reputation like his?

   Helping others

4. In what ways does deception harm the church? In what ways does it harm our reputation as Christians in the world?

   Prevents Holy Spirit from working effectively

5. Can you think of anything the government asks you to do that is a sin? (Be careful to distinguish what the government *allows* and what it *requires*.) Can you think of examples in other countries where the government asks its citizens to sin? What would you do if that were the case in your country?

6. Have you ever thought of persecution as a blessing? In what ways do your trials help you identify with Christ (1 Peter 4:13)? Give an example.

7. Have you ever complained about your church? What happened? Reflect on this question: "Would a perfect church have me as a member?"

Part 2
Stephen Is Martyred and Christianity Spreads
Acts 6:8–9:31

The church's appointment of the seven men to administer the widows' food program was no trivial matter. It was God-ordained. In His sovereignty, God moved through the apostles to choose seven men, none of whom have a Jewish name, and one—Nicolas—who is a Gentile convert to the Jewish faith. As we will see in part 2 of Acts, God is setting the stage for His message to go beyond Jerusalem and the religious borders of Judaism.

You see, the Jews had always considered themselves to be God's *chosen* people, which to them meant *exclusive*. They didn't believe God had any use for non-Jews, commonly known as Gentiles. How wrong they were. God's offer of salvation is for the whole world. In the next two chapters, God uses Stephen to prepare the way by dramatically communicating that message, and then God chooses Paul to carry it to the world.

Chapter 4

The Story of Stephen

Acts 6:8–7:60

What's Ahead

☐ Stephen Is Arrested (6:8-15)

☐ Stephen Preaches (7:1-53)

☐ Stephen Is Martyred (7:54-60)

For the Jews, nothing was more sacred and precious than the Law and the Temple.

- The *Law* was given to God's people and could never be changed.

- The *Temple* was the only place where sacrifices could be offered and God could truly be worshipped.

When Stephen, a Greek-speaking Jew, begins to challenge their traditions and beliefs by preaching that the Law is only a stepping-stone to the person and message of Christ, and that God doesn't live in the Temple, they get more than a little upset.

Stephen Is Arrested (6:8-15)

Some Jews attempt to debate Stephen, but they are no match for him. So they begin a campaign of lies, saying that Stephen spoke blasphemy against Moses and God. This riles the crowd, the elders, and the religious teachers, who promptly arrest Stephen and bring him before the council. There the "witnesses" repeat their lies—in fact they embellish them—by saying that Stephen is against the Law and the Temple.

Who Was Stephen?

We know from the first half of Acts 6 that Stephen is one of seven men chosen by the apostles for administrative duties. Specifically, he is a man "full of faith and the Holy Spirit" (6:5). Now we learn in just one verse (6:8) that Stephen possesses several character qualities that truly set him apart as a man chosen by God for this unique time in the history of the church. He is full of God's grace, full of God's power, a miracle worker, and an expert debater.

Have you ever been the object of a campaign of lies? Do you know someone who has? It's not uncommon, especially with issues concerning God and the Bible. When the opponents of truth are unable to successfully enter into the debate—in other words, when they can't win the argument using truth and reason—they will often resort to lying.

Stephen has discovered the truth and reality of Jesus Christ, who has changed him from the inside out. And now, as he stands before his accusers, the inner light of Jesus comes through him so that his face becomes "as bright as an angel's." Our faces may not physically shine like that, but the light of Christ and the power of the Holy Spirit in us should change our countenance, our attitude, and our actions so that when people encounter us, they can sense the glory of God. Paul refers to this transformation:

> *And as the Spirit of the Lord works within us,*
> *we become more and more like him and reflect*
> *his glory even more* (2 Corinthians 3:18).

Stephen Preaches (7:1-53)

The high priest asks Stephen just one question: "Are these accusations true?" And Stephen responds with the longest recorded message in Acts. Some commentators call this "Stephen's defense," but he isn't really trying to defend himself. Stephen takes the offense by carefully explaining the Gospel. Stephen has to know that he's on thin ice by telling the Sanhedrin that they are far from the truth. The apostles had almost been executed for using this approach, so is Stephen signing his own death certificate? Maybe, but he is doing so willingly. For Stephen, speaking the truth is far more important than living. As for living or dying, Stephen knows he will come out a winner either way: If they accept the truth, then he lives; if they don't, he still has Jesus.

> He is no fool who gives up what he cannot keep to gain what he cannot lose.
>
> —*Jim Elliot,*
> *twentieth-century*
> *martyred missionary*

Stephen's Three-Point Message

Stephen is a smart guy who was also filled with wisdom and the Holy Spirit (an unbeatable combination). He probably knows the history of the Jews and God's relationship with them better than the religious leaders do. Whereas his accusers see Old Testament history from a *legalistic* perspective, Stephen sees it from a *prophetic* viewpoint. He knows that Jesus was the fulfillment of the Law and Old Testament prophecy. Watch as Stephen lays out a masterful three-point message that defines the issues and tells his accusers exactly where they've gone wrong.

Point #1: God's program progresses and changes. The Jewish leaders held firmly to the belief that traditions don't change because God always works the same way (they believed this in order to keep their powerful positions). Through his razor-sharp grasp of history, Stephen gives them three examples of how God has been creative and innovative when dealing with people, especially the people of Israel.

- *Abraham* (7:2-8)—God called the father of the Jewish nation out of his native land in order to go to a new land.

- *Joseph* (7:9-16)—The brothers of this favorite son sold him into slavery in Egypt, where God delivered him and gave him favor before Pharaoh.

- *Moses* (7:17-43)—The deliverer of Israel was born in Egypt, was exiled in Midian, and then led God's people out of slavery.

The spirit of adventure of these three patriarchs, so important to the Jewish nation, stands in contrast to the entrenched and stubborn Jews in Jerusalem, who hated change. In fact, that's why they feel so threatened by

Jesus. As Barclay writes, the Jews who accused Stephen saw Jesus and His followers as "dangerous innovators."

Stephen also shows how God designed the Tabernacle to be portable and temporary (7:44-45). As for the Temple, he uses the words of the great prophet Isaiah to remind them that it was never meant to be God's home but rather was built to symbolize His presence (7:46-50).

Point #2: The blessings of God are not limited to the land of Israel and the Temple. The religious leaders believed their land was the only place where God could bless His people. Stephen contradicts this by giving four examples:

- God blessed Israel's patriarchs outside the land of Israel.

  ✓ God appeared to Abraham in Mesopotamia (7:2).

  ✓ God was with Joseph in Egypt (7:9).

  ✓ God commissioned Moses in Midian (7:29-34).

- The Law was given outside the land (7:38).

- The Tabernacle was built in the desert (7:44).

- The Temple transcends any one place (7:48-50).

Point #3: Israel has a history of opposing God's message and His messengers. This is the most scathing part of Stephen's indictment. Stephen gives some examples:

- Joseph was sold into slavery by his brothers (7:9).

- Their ancestors rejected Moses (7:39).

And then he ends his message with a flourish, telling these "stubborn people" that their ancestors killed the prophets, who predicted the coming of Jesus into the world, and then they betrayed and killed the Messiah Himself.

Stephen Is Martyred (7:54-60)

The council chamber erupts as the Jewish leaders shake their fists in rage. A lynch mob (or in this case, a stoning mob) quickly forms. They're not going to let this blasphemer get away with his accusations. This time Gameliel's not there to bring reason and order to the proceedings. Suddenly, in the midst of the bedlam, this holy man who is full of the Holy Spirit has an astounding vision of heaven.

Look, I See the Heavens Opened (7:55-57)

Stephen gazes up toward heaven and declares, "Look, I see the heavens opened and the Son of Man standing in the place of honor at God's right hand!" Stephen's vision is not the hallucination of a madman. Luke's language isn't symbolic. What Stephen sees is very real—for him and for us. He really is looking into heaven itself. We've heard reports firsthand of modern-day saints who, on their deathbed, look upward and speak of seeing Jesus or an angel as they pass from this life to the next. We need to remember that this life is but a shadow of the next, and as redeemed believers our true home is in heaven with Jesus. Paul gives us this advice:

> Since you have been raised to new life with Christ, set your sights on the realities of heaven, where Christ sits at God's right hand in the place of honor and power. Let heaven fill your thoughts. Do not think only about things down here on earth (Colossians 3:1-2).

Two things about Stephen's vision are worth noting:

- *Jesus is standing at God's right hand.* In many other Scriptures, Jesus is *seated* at the Father's right hand (Psalm 110:1; Romans 8:34; Colossians 3:1; Hebrews 12:2; 1 Peter 3:22). This is the only instance where Jesus is *standing* at God's right hand. Why? Because He is welcoming Stephen into heaven!

- *Stephen refers to Jesus as "the Son of Man."* This is the last time this term for Jesus is used in the New Testament, and it is the only time anyone besides Jesus uses it. (It was the title Jesus most often used to describe Himself.) Stephen's use of "Son of Man" shows that Jesus is the Messiah. (This was not lost on the religious leaders, by the way.) It comes from Daniel 7:13-14, and when combined with Psalm 110:1, it shows that Christ isn't just a ruler for the Jews but the ruler and Savior of the world.

Lord, Don't Charge Them with This Sin (7:58-60)

In their blindness to the truth, the religious leaders are convinced that Stephen has committed blasphemy (that is, speaking irreverently about God), the punishment for which is death by stoning (Leviticus 24:14). So they drag him out of the city and begin to stone him. Notice the two things Stephen says as they are in the process of killing him: "Lord Jesus, receive my spirit," and "Lord, don't charge them with this sin!"

Sound familiar? It should. Those were almost the exact words Jesus used as He was dying on the cross:

Jesus	Stephen
Father, I entrust my spirit into your hands! (Luke 23:46).	*Lord Jesus, receive my spirit* (Acts 7:59).
Father, forgive these people, because they don't know what they are doing (Luke 23:34).	*Lord, don't charge them with this sin!* (Acts 7:60).

Like his Lord, Stephen dies at peace with God, himself and the world—even his enemies.... By showing us how to die, he also shows us how to live and models the secret staying power of Christian witness even to death. If he can die for his Lord like that, confidently, forgiving his enemies, there must be something to this Jesus who he says reigns at God's right hand.

—*William J. Larkin Jr.*

If you wonder whether or not God answered Stephen's prayer, just look at Saul, the only "adversary" named in this story of Stephen. As Saul, he was one of the church's strongest persecutors, and yet he would soon become Paul, its greatest missionary. As Augustine said, "The Church owes Paul to the prayer of Stephen."

■ ■ ◩

Study the Word

1. What can you do when other people tell lies about you? How should you respond to those who are telling the lies? What should you say to those who are hearing the lies?

2. Have you ever known someone who was so filled
    with the light of Christ and the power of the Holy
    Spirit that their countenance reflected the glory of
    God? Describe the person and the impact he or she
    had on others.

3. Stephen had such passion for the truth of Jesus
    Christ that he was willing to die for it. Can we share
    his passion for the truth even though our lives aren't
    on the line? Explain how you could have a passion
    for the truth when something like your reputation is
    at stake.

4. In his Gospel, Luke records a parable that Jesus told
    to the religious leaders about a farmer who planted a
    vineyard, leased it out to tenant farmers, and sent his
    servants to collect his share of the crop at harvest-
    time. Read the parable in Luke 20:9-19. Identify
    these characters in the story. In other words, whom
    was Jesus referring to when He talked about...

    • the owner of the vineyard

    • the tenant farmers

    • the servants

    • the son

    • others

5. How can you "let heaven fill your thoughts"? (See Hebrews 12:1-3.) Why are we so easily distracted by and preoccupied with earthly things?

6. Read the following verses about Jesus at the right hand of God: Psalm 110:1; Romans 8:34; Hebrews 12:2; and 1 Peter 3:22. What can you learn about what Jesus is doing at God's right hand? What is His position?

Chapter 5

The Ministry of Philip and the Conversion of Saul

Acts 8:1–9:31

What's Ahead

- Persecution Scatters the Church (8:1-4)
- The Ministry of Philip (8:5-40)
- The Conversion of Saul (9:1-19)
- Saul's New Life (9:20-31)

From the Roman rulers in the first century to the atheistic despots in our own time, tyrants have always believed they could silence the witness of Christ by persecuting His followers. The religious leaders in Jerusalem certainly think the news of Stephen's death will quiet the believers and put an end to the rapid growth of the church. But they are wrong, just as all those who think they can crush the cause of Christ are wrong. Rather than suppress the message of Christ, persecution encourages it to spread. Tertullian, a prolific Christian apologist who lived in Northern Africa in the second and third centuries, said this to the rulers of the Roman Empire:

Kill us, torture us, condemn us, grind us to the dust....The more you mow us down, the more we grow. The seed is the blood of Christians.

We're about to see how the blood of Stephen becomes the seed of growth for the church.

Persecution Scatters the Church (8:1-4)

The martyrdom of Stephen has a stunning effect on both the persecutors and the believers. A new wave of persecution begins on the very day of Stephen's death.

Judea and Samaria (8:1-2)

When the heat gets turned up in Jerusalem, the believers flee into Judea and Samaria. Those places prob-ably sound familiar—Jesus mentioned them specifically in His great commission (1:8). The church in Jerusalem is growing rapidly, but so far nothing much is happening in the rest of Judea and in Samaria. Again, we see God's sovereignty at work. He doesn't cause the perse-cution (God is inca-pable of causing or doing evil), but He uses it for His glory. Who 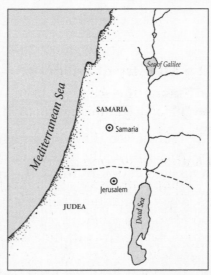 knows how long the believers would have taken to leave the nest of Jerusalem? But they had to spread the word, and the sudden spark of persecution is the key.

Saul the Persecutor (8:3-4)

Notice that the apostles stay behind as the others flee. That's probably because Saul is on the warpath. He's like a raging bull, dragging Christians out of their homes, beating them (Acts 22:19), and throwing them into jail. The church is in turmoil and needs the leadership to stay in place. The believers who go into Judea and Samaria are more like missionaries than refugees because they immediately begin to preach the Good News about Jesus.

Scattered Believers

The word *fled* in 8:1 and 8:4 (NLT) is better translated "scattered" (NIV, NASB) because the Greek word has the meaning of "sowing seed." The seeds of the Gospel are literally being sown as these believers are scattered.

The Ministry of Philip (8:5-40)

Among the scattered believers is Philip, one of the seven food administrators (6:5). Philip is a compelling preacher who also performs many miracles.

Miracles in Samaria (8:5-8)

Philip's ministry and miracles in Samaria brought great joy. Some preachers today believe that signs and wonders and miracles should characterize their ministries. Because this attitude is not uncommon in our day (especially on television), we want to make a couple of observations. First, we need to understand the purpose of the so-called "sign gifts" in the early church. R.C. Sproul writes, "Miracles were designed primarily to verify the credibility of the apostolic witness." J. Vernon McGee adds, "By the time the canon of Scripture was complete and established, the credentials of a true man of God was correct doctrine rather than sign gifts."

What that means is that since the time of the apostles, the preaching of the Word has been the most important part of evangelism. The early church had only the Old Testament Scriptures. They didn't have the book of Romans or the Gospel of John or any of the other New Testament Scriptures, so the Holy Spirit worked through signs and wonders to authenticate the apostles' message. That's not to say that God is no longer in the miracle business. He most certainly is! But when signs and wonders become the focal point of a ministry, we need to be careful.

Simon the Great (8:9-13)

Philip wasn't the only miracle worker in Samaria. Meet Simon, "The Great One," or as we like to call him, Simon the Sorcerer. This guy has a neat little business of doing magic tricks for profit. Then along comes Philip, whose miracles are by the power of the Holy Sprit rather than demons, and suddenly Simon isn't so great anymore. (Let this be a lesson: God's truth will always win out over Satan's lies.) Simon isn't stupid, so he figures, "If you can't beat 'em, join 'em!" He believes and is baptized.

> Dr. Stanley Toussaint defines *sorcery* as "the ability to exercise control over nature and/or people by means of demonic power."

The Holy Spirit Can't Be Bought (8:14-25)

But something isn't right. Simon follows Philip around, but he's preoccupied by the miracles. Finally,

Simon figures out where this special power is coming from. Peter and John have come from Jerusalem to Samaria in order to pray for the Holy Spirit to come upon these new Christians. Simon observes this and decides he has to have the Holy Spirit too. So he offers Peter and John some money to have access to their power. Peter sees exactly what is happening and tells Simon that he's full of it (*it* meaning bitterness and sin).

This section of Scripture raises a couple of questions:

1. *Why didn't the people in Samaria receive the Holy Spirit as soon as they believed?*

   The new believer is normally baptized into the body of Christ at the moment of conversion (1 Corinthians 12:13), but this wasn't normal. These new believers in Samaria received a special blessing in order to authenticate the Gospel message. Some scholars refer to this as the "Samaritan Pentecost."

2. *Was Simon really saved, or was he just faking it?*

   Only God knows who has genuinely repented and is saved (2 Timothy 2:19), so we need to be careful about questioning the spiritual condition of others. Still, Simon's case is instructive. Stanley Toussaint gives several reasons to doubt the genuineness of Simon's conversion experience. First, Simon's faith could have been like that of the demons in James 2:19. He merely believed in God, but didn't believe God's message. Second, faith based only on signs and wonders is not trustworthy (John 2:23-25). Third, Luke never tells us that Simon received the Holy Spirit. Fourth, the fact that Simon is "full of bitterness and held captive by sin" (Acts 8:23) would indicate that he never repented.

Philip and the Ethiopian (8:26-40)

Just when we think we can't relate to these first-century evangelists, with their miracles and powerful preaching, we read about a close encounter between Philip and an Ethiopian. This story shows us how one-on-one witnessing should be done. Notice three key things present in this story: the Holy Spirit (8:29), the Word of God (8:30-34), and the proclamation of the Word (8:35).

Based on these key elements, the story of Philip and the Ethiopian gives us several guidelines as we witness to friends, family, neighbors, coworkers, and even strangers.

- *We need to be responsive to God's call.* As we walk in fellowship with God (by spending daily time in prayer and God's Word, and by confessing our sins to God), we are going to experience the still, small voice of the Holy Spirit, encouraging us to talk with certain individuals about the life-transforming message of Christ. We need to respond to this call.

- *We don't have to wonder if people are "ready" to hear the Gospel.* We need to understand that God is the One who prepares the heart to receive His message.

- *We need to know the Word of God.* The Holy Spirit works through God's Word much more than He does through our personalities or good intentions.

- *We need to proclaim the Word of God*, not by preaching but by asking and answering questions. Peter writes, "And if you are asked about your Christian hope, always be ready to explain it" (1 Peter 3:15). This implies that people will ask us questions about our faith. We need to give them the opportunity to do just that.

- *We need to keep Jesus at the center.* Every religion includes Jesus in one way or another (great prophet, wise teacher, etc.), but only Christianity has Him at the center. Christianity is nothing without the risen Lord (1 Corinthians 15:14-19).

The Conversion of Saul (9:1-9)

Now we come to the most famous conversion story in the book of Acts. Saul the persecutor, who is on his way to Damascus to arrest more Christians, has a dramatic encounter with the risen Christ.

Saul Sees the Light (9:1-9)

Did Saul actually meet Jesus on the road to Damascus? Absolutely. Here we read that Saul heard the voice of the Lord, and later he writes that he saw Jesus with his own eyes (1 Corinthians 9:1). Because he *saw* and *heard* the resurrected Lord, he could legitimately call himself an apostle.

The effect of Saul's encounter with Christ is immediate and unmistakable. Just moments before, Saul was snarling on his way to Damascus. Now he is being led by the hand like a child.

God's Chosen Instrument (9:10-19)

Jesus tells Saul to continue to Damascus, where he would be told what to do. Of course, this implies that someone is going to tell him. That someone is Ananias, who certainly isn't expecting to meet with the church's chief persecutor. But the Lord has other ideas, so He tells

Ananias in a vision that he is to do two things: Lay hands on Saul so he can see again, and tell him that he is to be God's chosen instrument. This is remarkable. The man who once held the coat of those who killed Stephen is going to take the message of Christ to Gentiles, kings, and the people of Israel.

How Much He Must Suffer for Me

When we witness to people, we usually don't tell them, "Oh, by the way, if you accept Jesus as your Lord and Savior, you're going to experience pain and suffering." No, we usually try to paint the best possible picture by saying something like "God loves you and has a wonderful plan for your life." It's true that a relationship with Christ has more benefits now than we can count, and God's plan for our eternal life in heaven is more wonderful than we can imagine. But along with the joy and wonder are trials and, for many Christians in other parts of the world, persecution. Why are we reluctant to talk about suffering? The Lord was up-front with what was going to happen to Paul. Why should we expect a smoother ride?

The fact is that suffering is part of the Christian life.

> Dear friends, don't be surprised at the fiery trials you are going through, as if something strange were happening to you. Instead, be very glad—because these trials will make you partners with Christ in his suffering, and afterward you will have the wonderful joy of sharing his glory when it is displayed to all the world (1 Peter 4:12-13).

We like the way Ajith Fernando puts it: "Not only does suffering deepen our tie with Christ, it also enhances the effectiveness of our ministry, especially the ministry of evangelism. This...is a message that ought to be emphasized in a world that seeks to avoid pain."

Saul's New Life (9:20-31)

What a strange sight for the believers in Damascus—this well-known enemy of the church is suddenly out in the streets preaching instead of persecuting!

A New Kind of Zeal (9:20-25)

Saul immediately uses his extensive training as a Pharisee to good advantage. He begins telling people in Damascus that Jesus is the Son of God—the Messiah they have been waiting for. Of course, this infuriates the Jews, so they resort to their old tactics and try to kill this man who used to be one of them. Some believers help Saul escape, and he heads for Jerusalem—eventually.

In his letter to the Galatian church, Paul explains that he "went away into Arabia," and not until "three years later" did he go to Jerusalem (Galatians 1:17-18). Scholars believe that Paul went to the Arabian Desert to spend time alone with God. He didn't rush into his public ministry but rather waited on the Lord until he was ready.

Saul's Encourager (9:26-31)

After Saul arrives in Jerusalem, he spends 15 days with Peter (Galatians 1:18), learning from this great apostle, and he tries to meet with the other believers. Understandably, they are skeptical. Saul needs a friend! Enter Barnabas the Encourager, who comes alongside Saul and becomes his friend and advocate. What a wonderful ministry encouragement can be. Because of the friendship and credibility of Barnabas, the apostles accept Saul, who begins to debate some Greek-speaking Jews (he was a tiger, wasn't he?). Once again, they are no match for the truth of the Gospel, and once again Saul's life is in danger, prompting the believers to ship their new partner in ministry to his hometown of Tarsus.

As this section closes, we see that the church has spread to Judea and Samaria, just as Jesus instructed.

> *The church then had peace throughout Judea, Galilee, and Samaria, and it grew in strength and numbers. The believers were walking in the fear of the Lord and in the comfort of the Holy Spirit* (Acts 9:31).

■ ■ ■

Study the Word

1. How can God not cause evil but use it for His glory? How do you personally reconcile the presence of evil in a world created by a holy God?

2. What happens when signs and wonders become the primary focus of a ministry? What are the short-term and long-term effects?

3. Some people believe you can lose your salvation, while others believe "once saved, always saved." How does the story of Simon the Sorcerer relate to the debate?

4. After hearing Philip tell him the Good News about Jesus, the Ethiopian wanted to be baptized. What happened to the Ethiopian between 8:35 and 8:36? How is water baptism different from baptism in the Spirit? Can water baptism save a person? Why or why not?

Peter told him the Good News about Jesus

5. Before Saul met the Lord on the road to Damascus, he was a high-ranking Pharisee. This meant that he had power and knowledge—probably the equivalent of a Ph.D. in Jewish law. If Saul was so well educated and so smart, why was he so ignorant about the truth of Jesus Christ? (See 1 Corinthians 1:18-25.)

1633

6. List at least three things we can learn from Ananias' response to God's call (9:10-19).

7. Describe the role of an encourager. What does it mean to be encouraged? Have you ever been an encourager to a specific person? Whom do you have in your life who encourages you?

*P*art 3

The Gospel Advances to the Gentiles

Acts 9:32–12:24

In the first two parts of Acts, we have seen how the church was born in Jerusalem and then spread to Judea and Samaria, following the instructions of Jesus. In part 3, we will see the Gospel expand to new places, but more importantly we're going to see the Good News message of Jesus Christ expand to a new people—the Gentiles. About six years have passed since Jesus died, came back to life, and ascended into heaven, yet the church is still almost exclusively Jewish. This is not the way God intends for it to be. His offer of salvation is for the whole world.

The Jews were always prejudiced against the Gentiles. The Jewish Christians, including Peter, the leader of the Jerusalem church, have the same prejudice. Peter obviously has a lot to learn about God's grace, and his lesson is about to start.

Chapter 6

The Church Expands Under Peter's Leadership

Acts 9:32–12:24

What's Ahead

- ☐ Peter Goes into Gentile Territory (9:32-43)

- ☐ An Entire Gentile Household Converts (10:1–11:18)

- ☐ The Church in Antioch (11:19-30)

- ☐ Persecution and a Jailbreak (12:1-24)

God really knows how to execute a plan. He doesn't just cram His will down our throats and demand that we respond. Instead, He creatively calls us to participate in a series of events and divinely ordained circumstances leading up to the effect He desires. Then, when the time is right, things happen just the way He planned. It's a thing of beauty.

When God spreads His message to the Gentiles, His creativity and sovereignty know no limit. Watch as He matches a reluctant leader with an eager follower in a huge spiritual breakthrough that has implications for us today.

1576

Peter Goes into Gentile Territory (9:32-43)

After focusing on Stephen, Philip, and Saul, Luke now turns his attention to Peter, who is visiting believers in various cities. In this section we see Peter heal a paralyzed man in Lydda and then raise a dead woman back to life in Joppa. Both of these coastal cities are 25 to 35 miles northwest of Jerusalem, and both contain a mixed population of Jews and Gentiles.

In Lydda Peter heals a man who's been paralyzed for eight years. Notice the language he uses to heal Aeneas (9:34). He copies the words Jesus used when He healed the lame man at the pool of Bethesda (John 5:8). The effect of Peter's healing on the town of Lydda is huge. Luke writes, "The whole population...turned to the Lord." This is an example of the Scriptures' use of hyperbole to make a point, and the point is that great numbers of people believed. (It would be the same as saying about a particular event, "Everybody was there.")

Evidently the news of the healing reaches Joppa, about ten miles to the north. The friends of Tabitha, a much-loved woman, send for Peter after she dies. They must think that after healing a paralyzed man, raising someone from the dead isn't that much of a stretch. Their faith is rewarded as Peter performs an astounding miracle, again copying the words of his Master, who once raised Jairus' daughter from the dead (Mark 5:41).

Once again the news has a great impact on the town, and many believe. Notice that Peter stays with a leatherworker named Simon. Because Simon worked with the skins of dead animals, most self-respecting Jews would not step foot into his home. Yet here's Peter enjoying Simon's hospitality. The barrier between Jew and Gentile is beginning to come down.

Love in Action

Tabitha was one of those Christians with a servant's heart who didn't crave the spotlight and went about her Kingdom business with grace and humility. She was always "doing kind things for others and helping the poor," and she made coats and clothes for the widows. What a true example of the love of Christ in action!

An Entire Gentile Household Converts (10:1–11:18)

The way God sets up His full-blown invasion of the Gospel into the Gentile world unfolds like a well-produced movie. The plot develops dramatically as God uses some choice weapons from His supernatural arsenal: visions, angels, and the Holy Spirit. And, as usual, He chooses to enlist ordinary people to accomplish His eternal purposes.

Cornelius Has a Vision (10:1-8)

The scene opens in Caesarea in the household of Cornelius, a Roman centurion and a pure-blooded Gentile. You'll never meet a more decent, moral, God-fearing, and generous man than Cornelius. Yet for all his virtues, he lacks one thing: He doesn't know the Lord Jesus Christ. Still, Cornelius is seeking the one true God. In His graciousness, God sends Cornelius a vision in which an angel tells him that God has heard his prayer. Immediately Cornelius sends a group of his men to get Peter.

Peter Has a Vision (10:9-16)

Meanwhile, back in Joppa, Peter is up on the roof praying. He falls into a trance (missing lunch), and God sends him a vision. In the vision, all kinds of animals are lowered from the sky on a sheet. God instructs Peter to kill and eat the critters, which flies in the face of what good Jews believe.

---

*M*orally *A*live but *S*piritually *D*ead

Have you ever known someone like Cornelius? People like this are all around us. They are faithful workers, they volunteer tirelessly to civic causes, they are generous, and they may even believe in God and attend a church. Yet they have never made a personal commitment to Christ. How does God view such people? First, we need to trust God that He is completely fair to all people. Second, we need to understand that good moral behavior won't save anyone. God's grace and our faith alone in Jesus Christ saves us (Ephesians 2:8-9). Third, we need to know that "God...rewards those who sincerely seek him" (Hebrews 11:6). God answered Cornelius' prayer by sending the right person at the right time with the right message.

Peter is "perplexed" after seeing this vision three times. (Peter always was a slow learner.) In fact, Peter disagrees with the Lord (something he's done before—see Matthew 16:23 and John 13:8). The point the Lord is making, of course, is that He is opening new doors for His message, and that means breaking down old barriers—in this case, dietary laws. Peter will soon learn that this vision applies to all aspects of the Jewish–Gentile relationship.

Peter Meets Cornelius (10:17-33)

Just as Peter's vision ends, the Cornelius delegation finds him and asks him to accompany them back to Caesarea. After a little more prodding by the Holy Spirit,

Peter and a group of believers travel to the house of this Gentile. When they arrive, a bunch of Cornelius' relatives and friends greet them. Don't you love this guy Cornelius? He's so eager and his heart is so tender. He even bows down to Peter out of respect, to which Peter replies, "Stand up! I'm a human being like you!" In other words, "We're all equal!"

More walls are coming down. God has prepared Cornelius' heart and softened Peter's, and the Holy Spirit is in full control. The greatest barrier to the spreading of God's Good News message—the barrier between Jews and Gentiles—is coming down.

Peter Preaches in Cornelius' House (10:34-43)

Peter continues with this theme of equality before God as he begins to preach: "God doesn't show partiality. In every nation he accepts those who fear him and do what is right" (10:34-35). From this point, Peter's sermon follows the tried-and-true format of the apostolic message, sometimes referred to as *kerygma* (the Greek word for *preaching*). This is essentially the same message he preached at Pentecost (2:14-36) and before the Sanhedrin (3:12-26).

---

*O*pen to *A*ll

Don't be misled or discouraged by people who claim that Christianity is an intolerant religion. Here is the fact: Christianity is wide open to all people of every stripe. Yes, we have only one way to God—by faith alone in Jesus Christ—but no one is excluded. The same cannot be said of other religions and belief systems that "pre-qualify" people either by what they do or who they are.

1578

Signs of Salvation (10:44-48)

We cannot possibly overestimate the importance of what took place in Cornelius' house that day. If you are a Gentile believer, you can trace your spiritual heritage to a first-century Roman centurion from Caesarea. Peter and the other Jewish believers certainly recognize how special this moment is, especially when three things immediately happen:

- *The Holy Spirit falls upon those who hear and believe.* The Holy Spirit's *immediate* work in the life of the new believer is the norm. It's a validation that the house of Cornelius is truly saved.

- *The new believers begin speaking in tongues.* Longe-necker writes that these tongues were likely "ecstatic utterances" (1 Corinthians 12–14) rather than the tongues of known languages that occurred at Pentecost.

- *The new believers begin praising God.* This is a nat-ural expression of a true convert.

1579

Peter Explains What Happened (11:1-18)

The news of the Gentile converts travels fast, but it isn't well received by the Jewish believers in Jerusalem. They don't mind that Peter had gone to a Gentile city to preach, but they don't like that he entered a Gentile house! Peter is in a bit of a tough spot, but he responds wisely, telling the skeptics everything that happened. By the end of his story, everyone is fully convinced.

We can learn from Peter and the way he handled the criticism. Rather than get defensive, he calmly and com-petently shares his vision, first by corroborating it with credible witnesses (11:12) and then by showing how the results of his vision were in agreement with what Jesus had said (11:16).

The Church in Antioch (11:19-30)

As soon as the church in Jerusalem accepts the Gentile converts, Christianity explodes into new Gentile frontiers, most notably Antioch of Syria.

A Thriving Church (11:19-26)

Next to Jerusalem, no city in the ancient world was more important to the cause of Christ than Antioch.

- The first Gentile church was founded in Antioch.

- Paul used Antioch as a base of operations for his missionary journeys.

- Believers were first called "Christians" in Antioch (11:26).

> The word *Christian* means "Christ follower" or "those of the household of Christ."

A Caring Church (11:27-30)

The church in Antioch demonstrates its character when Agabus prophesies that a famine is coming to the Roman world. The believers take this seriously and raise money for the mother church. They entrust Saul and Barnabas with taking the relief fund to Jerusalem.

Persecution and a Jailbreak (12:1-24)

As part 3 of Acts winds to a close, we're going to see two examples of God working on behalf of the church.

King Herod's Reign of Terror (12:1-5)

Like most kings under Roman rule, Herod Agrippa's main goal is to keep the peace (his job depends on it). He views the Jewish Christians as divisive, so to make a point he begins to persecute some believers and has James killed (this is the apostle James, the brother of John). Then he goes after Peter, throwing him in jail with plans to execute him after Passover.

All in the Family

King Herod Agrippa comes from a long line of wicked Herods. A grandfather, Herod the Great, ruled Palestine when Jesus was born and was responsible for the extermination of all boys under the age of two (Matthew 2:16). An uncle, Herod Antipas, was involved in the trial of Jesus (Luke 23:7-12) and the death of John the Baptist (Mark 16:14-29).

Peter's Miraculous Escape (12:6-19)

Peter's escape from prison reads like a scene from a sitcom. We don't mean to make light of a very serious situation, but the way Peter and the angel walked out of the jail is hilarious. The comedy continues when Peter shows up at the home of Mary, John Mark's mother (John Mark is the cousin of Barnabas). He's left standing at the door while the believers, who have been praying for him, refuse to believe he's broken out of jail.

Perhaps this story strikes a chord with us because we can identify with the Christians gathered in Mary's house. How often have we earnestly prayed for something or someone, only to overlook the results because we lack faith?

1581

God Takes Care of Herod (12:20-24)

Not only does God have a sense of humor, but he also knows how to deliver poetic justice. When Herod takes himself too seriously and "accept[s] the people's worship instead of giving glory to God," an angel afflicts him with a deadly disease, effectively removing Herod and his evil ways from the scene. Another obstacle to the Great Commission falls, and the church continues to grow.

> *But God's Good News was spreading rapidly,*
> *and there were many new believers*
> (Acts 12:24).

■ ■ ■

Study the Word

1. God speaks to people in many different ways. He spoke to Cornelius and Peter through visions. More commonly, God speaks to people today through the Scriptures, other people, preachers, circumstances, and events. How did God first speak to you?

1-1-89

2. Peter wasn't the only one to have an encounter with a Roman centurion. Jesus had a conversation with a centurion (Luke 7:1-10), and a centurion was present at the crucifixion (Mark 15:37-39). What do these passages about centurion encounters tell you about God's attitude toward the military?

1483

3. Suppose you were asked to prepare a message based on Peter's *kerygma* in 10:34-43. What would be your main points?

   God doesn't show partiality

4. The Jewish believers in Jerusalem criticized Peter before they had the facts about the conversion of Cornelius. Give two reasons why this type of criticism is destructive rather than constructive. What can we learn from the way Peter handled it?

5. What did Barnabas do once he arrived at Antioch (11:22-25)? Why do you think he went to Tarsus to get Saul?

   See footnotes 1579

6. No doubt the believers prayed for James with as much faith as they prayed for Peter, and yet James died and Peter didn't. Why do you think God chose to spare Peter but not James? Did God answer the prayers for both men? In what ways?

$\mathcal{P}$art 4

Paul's First Missionary Journey
Acts 12:25–16:5

Something like 15 years have passed since Jesus gave His commission to reach the world. Remarkably, in that relatively short period of time, the church in Jerusalem has carried out Christ's instructions throughout Judea and Samaria. The Gospel has broken through the barrier between Jews and Gentiles and has crossed into other cultures as well. All that remains is to take the Good News message "to the ends of the earth."

In God's providence, Saul (soon to be renamed Paul) will be the one to spearhead the last part of the global assignment. In one sense, the rest of Acts—from Paul's first missionary journey in Acts 13 to his trip to Rome in Acts 28—is all about taking the Gospel to the rest of the world. Yet even as Acts closes, the story is not finished because the job is not done. Two thousand years later, we are still telling the story by doing what Christ called us to do.

Let's learn from those early years, when the church expanded to more and more diverse cultures, established first-rate mission strategies, and conquered the spiritual forces of darkness—all in the power of the Holy Spirit.

Chapter 7

Paul's First Missionary Journey

Acts 12:25–14:28

What's Ahead

- The Missionaries Are Sent (12:25–13:13)
- Paul's Sermon in the Synagogue (13:14-41)
- First to the Jews—Then to the Gentiles (13:42-52)
- Iconium, Lystra, and Derbe (14:1-28)

Back in the beginning of this study, we stated that Acts is a book of *action*. With relentless forward movement, the church preaches the Gospel in ever widening circles. The action is going to continue, but the main characters are going to change. So far Luke's narrative has focused on Peter and the Jerusalem church. Now the attention shifts to Paul, God's chosen instrument of Jesus "to take my message to the Gentiles and to kings, as well as to the people of Israel" (9:15).

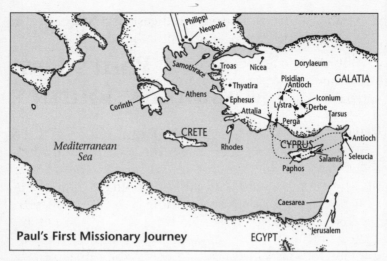

Paul's First Missionary Journey

The Missionaries Are Sent (12:25–13:13)

1581   Having delivered the relief funds to Jerusalem, Saul and Barnabas return to Antioch of Syria, taking John Mark with them.

The Rainbow Coalition (12:25–13:1)

Luke gives a list of the "prophets and teachers" of the church at Antioch, and it's fascinating to see who's included:

- *Barnabas*—the great encourager himself, who is a Jew from Cyprus

- *Simeon*—a dark-skinned man, probably from Northern Africa

- *Lucius*—a Roman, also from Africa

- *Manaen*—a foster brother of King Herod Antipas, which indicates he is of high social standing

- *Saul*—a Pharisee from southeast Asia Minor and a former persecutor of the church

Talk about cultural, ethnic, and geographic diversity! The church at Antioch is a model of what the church should look like. The body of Christ is open to all.

Dedicated to the Lord (13:2-3)

The Holy Spirit tells the leadership at Antioch to "dedicate" Barnabas and Saul for special service. (Notice that the Holy Spirit speaks with authority equal to Jesus. The Holy Spirit and Jesus are distinct from each other, but both are God.) To *dedicate* means to "set apart." To this day we dedicate our pastors, missionaries, and special workers for the job God has called them to do. In the same way, we need to dedicate ourselves—that is, set ourselves apart—to carry out the work God has called us to do.

Do You Feel Called?

Have you been "called" by God to do a special work for Him? William Larkin says the call of God on your life includes two aspects: (1) an inward call that only you can sense, and (2) an outward confirmation through the church. An inward call without outward confirmation may not be the real thing. If you feel called, discuss it with your pastor or other leaders in your church. Trust the Holy Spirit to speak to them as surely as He has spoken to you.

A Governor Believes (13:4-13)

Saul and Barnabas, assisted by John Mark, travel to the island of Cyprus. Why Cyprus? First of all, they have been sent by the Holy Spirit. But they have other practical considerations. Cyprus is a key population and cultural center, it's along a well-traveled route, and it contains a synagogue. Once again God is preparing the way!

Right away the team heads to the synagogue, where they begin to preach. They then journey more than 100 miles (on foot, mind you) to the other side of the island, where they meet Bar-Jesus, a Jewish sorcerer who serves as a kind of spiritual advisor to the governor. (*Bar* means "son of," so this guy was the son of a man named Jesus—or Joshua—a common name in those days.)

The governor is a man of "considerable insight and understanding" who wants to hear the Word of God, but this smarmy sorcerer has attached himself to his employer like a leech and tries to interfere with the Christian witness. Clearly this is spiritual warfare in action. This is not the last time the "evil rulers and authorities of the unseen world" (Ephesians 6:12) are going to harass the missionaries in Acts. Satan and his forces of darkness are dead set on disrupting the activities of God's people as they witness for Christ. They can even worm their way into high places, influencing leaders to ignore the truth.

Paul, filled with the Holy Spirit, confronts this "son of the Devil" (just the opposite of his name) and strikes him blind. The governor's eyes are opened, however, and he believes in the Lord Jesus Christ. We shouldn't be surprised, and we shouldn't worry when we face spiritual warfare. The apostle John bolsters our confidence:

> *But you belong to God, my dear children. You have already won your fight with these false prophets, because the Spirit who lives in you is greater than the spirit who lives in the world* (1 John 4:4).

From Saul to Paul

From this point forward, Luke will refer to Saul (his Hebrew name) as Paul (his Roman name). Paul himself was using his Roman name as he moved into Gentile regions to preach the Gospel. In addition, Paul probably identified with the meaning of "Paul"—"small" or "little" (see Philippians 3:7-8).

Paul's Sermon in the Synagogue (13:14-41)

Paul and Barnabas now travel to Antioch of Pisidia (different from Antioch of Syria) and again make the synagogue their first stop. Synagogue leaders customarily invited visiting rabbis to speak. Paul takes advantage of this custom by addressing the "people of Israel" and "devout Gentiles." (Had the locals known that Paul was going to speak about Jesus the Messiah, they never would have given him the podium!)

Paul begins his message by emphasizing God's covenant with Israel. Paul was a master at relating to his audiences. As he would later write, "Yes, I try to find common ground with everyone so that I might bring them to Christ" (1 Corinthians 9:22). We need to learn from Paul by finding common ground with the people we talk with—one person or a large group—before we share Christ with them.

The focus of Paul's message is 13:38-39:

> Brothers, listen! In this man Jesus there is forgiveness for your sins. Everyone who believes in him is freed from all guilt and declared right with God—something the Jewish law could never do.

There it is! The heart of the Good News of Jesus Christ. Forgiveness of sins is ours through Jesus Christ. Paul will repeat this core message of justification by faith alone countless times in his witnessing to commoners and kings. Like Paul, we need to present the Gospel in a clear, concise, and correct manner.

A Warning for Everyone

At the end of his message, Paul issues this warning: Be careful! Don't miss this opportunity to have your sins forgiven. The law—that is, your own good deeds—cannot save you. Only faith alone in Jesus can make you right with God. This warning is not just for the legalistic Jewish leaders but for all who think they are good enough to meet God's requirements.

First to the Jews—Then to the Gentiles (13:42-52)

The response of the people who hear Paul's message in the synagogue is electric. By the end of the following week, "almost the entire city" comes to hear Paul and Barnabas preach the Word. As always—and this hasn't changed—the preaching of the Word, with Jesus as the central theme, is the key to effective evangelism.

The Jewish leaders are jealous of the crowds, but something deeper is probably going on. According to Richard Longenecker, they are agitated that Paul is offering the "sacred blessings" (13:34) of God to the Gentiles without requiring that they become Jews first. Evidently this is the case because Paul and Barnabas address the issue in 13:46. Essentially they tell the Jewish leaders, "Look, we offered this Good News from God to you guys first, but you rejected it, and you're still rejecting it. So we're offering it to the Gentiles, and they're loving it!" Paul even quotes from their own prophet Isaiah, who predicted that Israel would be a light to the Gentiles (Isaiah 49:6). These Jewish leaders are too blinded and stubborn to realize that prophecy was fulfilled in Jesus, who came through Israel as a light to the world (John 8:12).

The Jewish leaders respond by organizing opposition among the influential religious women and the leaders of the city, who end up running Paul and Barnabas out of town. This type of action against the Christian message is common to this day. In fact, with the rise of political correctness and religious pluralism in this country, Christianity is increasingly viewed as intolerant and disruptive. Don't be surprised when community leaders speak out against the public expression of Christian beliefs.

Iconium, Lystra, and Derbe (14:1-28)

After shaking the dust of Antioch of Pisidia off their feet, Paul and Barnabas travel about 90 miles southeast to Iconium and then on to Lystra and Derbe. These three cities are located in the southern part of Galatia, a region in what is present-day Turkey. Paul's experiences in Galatia eventually led to him writing the first of his nine letters (or *epistles*) to churches. J. Vernon McGee calls the book of Galatians "the harshest epistle that Paul wrote." The people of Galatia were tough customers, spiritually speaking.

Preaching Boldly in Iconium (14:1-7)

As usual, Paul and Barnabas start their missionary efforts at the synagogue. As usual, many believe. As usual, opposition builds, this time from Jews and Gentiles alike. Preaching "boldly about the grace of God," the apostles hang in there for a long time. This strength in the face of opposition can only come from the Holy Spirit. Notice that God gives them the power to do signs and wonders in order to prove the message. Here's the pattern: Preaching the Gospel always takes the lead; signs and wonders play a supporting role.

Drama in Lystra (14:8-20)

Once again, the signs and wonders—this time the miracle of healing a man born lame from birth—follow the preaching. Realizing the lame man had faith, Paul healed him, causing the locals to refer to Barnabas and Paul as Zeus and Hermes. Our two intrepid missionaries are absolutely shocked (maybe they remembered what happened to Herod when the people called him a god). They tear their clothes and run into the crowd, telling them, "We are merely human beings like yourselves!" Paul then addresses the crowd with a very interesting message.

Clinton Arnold observes that Paul is preaching to Gentiles who have no knowledge of Scripture, so he frames his message in terms they can understand. Drawing from the natural world to make a case for belief in "the living God," he pleads with them to turn from their idolatry of dead, worthless beings. Well, these false-god worshippers don't want to hear that. Incited by some out-of-town Jews, they turn on Paul and nearly kill him.

From Derbe Back to Antioch (14:1-28)

God not only preserves Paul but also gives him a miraculous recovery! The next day Paul and Barnabas go to Derbe, and then they turn around and retrace their steps back through Lystra and Iconium, to Antioch of Pisidia. Even though they had been kicked out of these cities, they assume the risk and take the time to strengthen the new believers (it's called "follow-up") and to remind them of the trials and tribulations ahead.

The first missionary journey of Paul and Barnabas ends where it began—in Antioch of Syria. They give a full report to the church, telling them that God has opened the "door of faith" to the Gentiles too. And just what is the door of faith? Why, it's Jesus!

> *I am the door; if anyone enters through Me, he will be saved, and will go in and out and find pasture* (John 10:9 NASB).

◼ ◼ ◼

Study the Word

1. William Larkin writes that the church in Antioch of Syria became a model for missionary vision, development, and support. List several characteristics of this pioneering church that support this view. (See 11:27-30; 13:1-3.)

   lead by spirit

   Rainbow Colition

   Preached to Gentiles as well as the Jews

2. In what way can you dedicate yourself to the Lord? What can you begin doing right now to set apart your...

    • time

    • talent

    • treasure

3. In most major cities in the ancient Near East, the synagogue was a major gathering place for Jews and devout Gentiles, so it proved to be a great place to preach the Word. Where do people gather in your city to discuss religion and philosophy? What can Christians do to gain access to these places?

4. Paul begins his message in the synagogue in Antioch of Pisidia with several principles from the Old Testament (known as the Old Testament *kerygma*). What are the main points of this part of Paul's message? (See 13:17-22.)

    Trying to find a common ground

5. How would you find common ground with the following people in order to share Christ with them?

 • a Muslim

 • a graduate student in philosophy

 • a contractor

 • your neighbor

6. What do you make of the phrase, "and all who were appointed to eternal life became believers" (13:48)? Compare this verse to the following passages: Romans 8:29-30; Ephesians 1:4-5; and 1 Peter 1:2. What do these verses have in common? As best as you can, explain the doctrine of election. (You get extra credit just for trying!)

7. Give an example of how a government agency or a civic leader might try to restrict evangelism in your community. What would you do if your school, your workplace, or your city government prevented you from expressing your beliefs in Christ?

Chapter 8

The Jerusalem Council

Acts 15:1–16:5

What's Ahead

- The Gentile Issue (15:1-4)

- Peter and James State the Case (15:5-21)

- Dear Gentiles (15:22-35)

- Paul's Second Missionary Journey (15:36–16:5)

*Y*ou will recall from the last chapter that the Jewish leaders opposed Paul because he was offering the blessings of God to the Gentiles without requiring that they become Jews first. That opposition came from the *outside*—these Jews had no interest or involvement in the church (to the contrary, they were very much against the church).

Now in this section of Acts we come to another kind of opposition, this time from the *inside*. A group of Jewish Christians—known as Judaizers—travels from Jerusalem to Antioch of Syria in order to convince the Christians there that Gentiles aren't really saved because

Who Are Judaizers?

Judaizers are devout, practicing Jews who believe in Jesus but hold to the notion that you can gain favor with God by keeping the law.

they haven't been circumcised. This is a very big issue that's going to require godly wisdom and diplomacy.

The Gentile Issue (15:1-4)

Here's the crux of the question raised by the Judaizers: Do Gentiles need to become Jews before they become Christians, or can they become part of the church without fulfilling the Jewish law? If we were considering this issue today in a wider context, we might state it this way: Is it necessary to add works to faith in Christ for salvation?

To Circumcise or Not to Circumcise...That Is the Question (15:1)

Clearly the Judaizers aren't saying the Gentiles can't be saved. They're saying the Gentiles are welcome in the church as long as they become Jews first. And the best way to demonstrate their commitment to Judaism is to "keep the ancient Jewish custom of circumcision taught by Moses." This refers to the covenant of circumcision God made with Abraham (Genesis 17), which served as a sign that the Jews were God's covenant people. More than any other ritual, the act of circumcision distinguished God's people from those who didn't follow God.

As you can imagine, this throws the Gentile Christians in Antioch for a loop. For one thing, it plants doubts in their minds about their own salvation. For another, it raises the rather unpleasant prospect that the men in the church may have to undergo a very painful procedure.

Let's Have a Conference (15:2-4)

Even more, this teaching by the Judaizers casts doubts on the very foundation of the Good News message of Christ. That's why Paul and Barnabas react so strongly. They agree that the Old Testament Law is important, but they are convinced that it cannot save and therefore is not required for salvation. The only way a person can be saved is through faith in Jesus Christ (13:38-39).

Paul and Barnabas argue long and hard with the Judaizers, prompting the church leaders to wisely appeal to the mother church in Jerusalem. They send a delegation of believers along with Paul and Barnabas to discuss the issue with the apostles and elders. The Jerusalem church welcomes the delegates from Antioch, who give them an encouraging report. The first conference in church history, officially known as the Jerusalem Council, is underway.

Contending for the Truth

We can disagree on minor doctrinal issues (such as the timing of the Tribulation or the way a church government should be structured), but when it comes to major doctrinal issues—such as the way we are saved—we need to respond to challenges the way Paul and Barnabas did and contend for the truth.

Peter and James State the Case (15:5-21)

The conference has just begun when some Judaizers stand up and declare that all Gentile converts must be circumcised. The big issue is on the table. After a long discussion, Peter addresses the group.

We Are All Saved the Same Way (15:5-12)

Peter frames the issue by asking this question: Can we truly be saved by earning God's favor? He answers it by telling the story of the conversion of Cornelius, a glorious event that occurred ten years earlier. Cornelius did nothing to earn God's favor. He and his household simply heard the Good News and believed. And God, who knows people's hearts, accepted their belief and confirmed it by giving them the Holy Spirit.

"Why are you now questioning God's way?" Peter asks. Adding conditions and requirements to salvation is like burdening people with a yoke that no one can bear. (A yoke was a heavy wooden harness used by oxen to pull heavy loads. In this context a yoke symbolizes religious obligation.) By contrast, the Good News is that salvation is available to all people "by the special favor of the Lord Jesus" (15:11).

Paul must have been taking notes, because in his letter to the Ephesians he would later write:

> God saved you by his special favor when you believed. And you can't take credit for this; it is a gift from God. Salvation is not a reward for the good things we have done, so none of us can boast about it (Ephesians 2:8-9).

How to Preserve Fellowship (15:13-21)

Peter, Paul, and Barnabas have all weighed in quite convincingly on the issue, but James, the leader of the Jerusalem church, hasn't given his opinion yet. Now it's his turn. James, the half brother of Jesus, stands up to deliver the final word and offer a solution to the controversy. He begins by affirming everything Peter has said about the Gentiles. He uses Scripture to show that God's salvation offer to the Gentiles is equal to God's saving acts toward Israel.

Legalism Today

Adding conditions and requirements to salvation—sometimes called *legalism*—is alive and well in the church today. We may not buy into the notion of salvation by works, but we can fall into the "performance trap" by doing certain things in order to get something back from God. As maturing believers we need to study the Scriptures, be involved in a church, pray regularly, and tell others about Jesus. But when we do these things with the expectation that God will bless us because we're doing things for Him, then we're putting our faith in a method rather than a Person. Remember, God is more interested in our hearts than our calendars or a spiritual to-do list.

James then makes two recommendations. One is doctrinal in nature, and the other is practical. The doctrinal recommendation is found in 15:19: "And so my judgment is that we should stop troubling the Gentiles who turn to God." His practical recommendation is found in 15:20, where he outlines four directives that have nothing to do with salvation but everything to do with preserving fellowship. James asks the Gentile converts to respect the Jewish Christians who still observe strict dietary laws. The way to do this is to simply abstain from eating things that would offend their Jewish brothers and sisters. He includes one non-dietary item—abstaining from sexual immorality—because the Jews are concerned about low moral standards among the Gentiles.

Too Legalistic?

On the surface James' practical recommendation appears to bring legalism back into the picture, but that's not the case at all. To the contrary, it highlights a principle that applies to this day, and here it is: If certain things we do offend other believers, even if we think they are being legalistic, then we need to refrain from doing those things in order to keep harmony. We may be free to eat whatever we want, but we aren't free to disrupt the body of Christ.

James' compromise is brilliant because it clearly affirms that we can do nothing to earn our salvation, and it recommends ways to preserve unity in the church. Larkin observes three things we can learn about getting along in a culturally diverse church:

1. We must not put any stumbling block in the way of the Gospel.

2. We must respect one another's differences and preferences.

3. We must use our freedom to *not* do what is permissible in other circumstances.

Dear Gentiles (15:22-35)

Now that the church has reached a decision, they have one more thing to do. They need to inform the Gentile believers in Antioch of Syria. They draft a letter and send it to the church in Antioch with a delegation that includes Paul and Barnabas and two other respected church leaders.

The Council's Letter (15:23-29)

The letter conveys the unanimous decision of the Jerusalem Council. It contains three major principles for the Gentile believers:

- You do not have to follow the external requirements of the law in order to be saved.

- Adjust your eating habits so you won't offend your Jewish brothers and sisters.

- Abstain from sexual immorality.

Wouldn't you agree that these principles apply to us today? Over the last 2000 years, human nature hasn't changed. People still have a tendency to add "performance conditions" to salvation. Peripheral issues will always have the potential to disrupt and divide the church. And sexual immorality is still a problem, even for believers.

Encouraged and Strengthened (15:30-35)

Look at the impact of the Jerusalem Council's recommendations on the believers in Antioch. There is "great joy throughout the church that day as they read this encouraging message." This is what happens when we "hold to the truth in love, becoming more and more in every way like Christ, who is the head of his body, the church" (Ephesians 4:15).

Paul's Second Missionary Journey (15:36–16:5)

After staying in Antioch for a while, Paul decides it's time for another road trip in order to follow up with the new converts. But first he and Barnabas have to settle a disagreement.

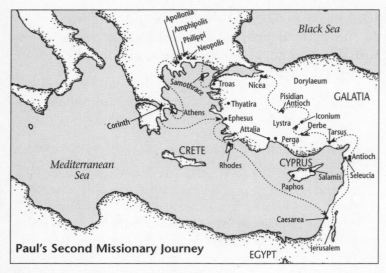

Paul's Second Missionary Journey

A Parting of the Ways (15:36-41)

Have you noticed that the Bible is a very honest book? As God directed the various authors to write His Word, He didn't sugarcoat anything. Notice how Luke reports the dispute that arose between Paul and Barnabas. It shows that even spiritual giants can disagree, but more importantly it shows just how lovingly our sovereign God takes care of us, flaws and all.

The issue here is that Barnabas wants to take his cousin, John Mark, on this second missionary journey, and Paul isn't about to let that happen. Paul thinks John Mark is a deserter (13:13). The disagreement between Paul and Barnabas is so intense that it splits the old team apart. The separation is amicable (the original language of Luke's text indicates that neither Paul nor Barnabas were blaming the other), but it seems damaging. Actually, that's only from the human standpoint. From God's sovereign perspective, this is an opportunity to create two teams and instantly double the impact of the Christian witness. Now you've got Barnabas and John Mark going to Cyprus *and* Paul and Silas traveling to Syria and Cilicia.

You Can Trust God

This story can teach us a huge lesson. We can trust God to use our setbacks for His glory. Don't be discouraged if something negative happens despite your best intentions. And here's another lesson: We can trust God to work in the lives of others even if we don't see their potential. Paul may have seen John Mark as a deserter, but God wasn't finished with him. God would later choose John Mark to write the story of His Son in the Gospel of Mark. And by the end of his ministry, Paul has come to appreciate Mark's helpfulness and loyalty (2 Timothy 4:11).

Teaching Others in the Lord (16:1-5)

Once again Paul returns to the cities where the young converts live. Paul is not one to "save 'em and leave 'em." He knows that new believers, who are tender and vulnerable, need the nourishment and teaching of more mature believers in order for their spiritual lives to properly take root.

Paul is delighted to find Timothy, a young disciple whom the other believers respected. Paul might have been looking for someone to take John Mark's place, but he was more likely wanting to teach and train someone to eventually take *his* place. "He was always well aware of the necessity of training a new generation for the work that lay ahead," William Barclay writes. "In Timothy he found just the kind of person he wanted." We know from Paul's writings that Timothy proved to be an outstanding learner (that's what a disciple is—a *learner*).

Paul referred to Timothy as "my beloved and trustworthy child in the Lord" (1 Corinthians 4:17).

We All Need a Paul, a Barnabas, and a Timothy

Dr. Howard Hendricks (affectionately known as "Prof" to his students) has always taught that each of us needs a Paul, a Barnabas, and a Timothy in our lives. We need a Paul to teach us, a Barnabas to encourage us, and a Timothy to learn from us. If you don't have people like that in your life right now, pray and ask God to lead you to them—and them to you!

Once again the church is on the move, and the stage is set for the next significant expansion of the Gospel.

> *So the churches were strengthened in their faith and grew daily in numbers* (Acts 16:5).

◼ ◼ ◼

Study the Word

1. In what ways do people try to add works to their salvation? Could this tendency keep somebody from being genuinely saved? How?

2. What are the things that plant doubt in your mind about your salvation? When these doubts occur, what do you do? What would you tell someone who wonders if they are really saved?

John 6 - 47
Mark 16 - 16

3. Read Matthew 23:4. What did Jesus say about religious obligation? Now read Matthew 11:28-30. What did Jesus say about carrying our burdens? How does His yoke differ from the yoke of obligation?

His yoke is easy

4. What are new believers most susceptible to? (In order to answer this question, read Jesus' parable about the farmer scattering seed in Luke 8:4-15.) Identify each of the following:

- the farmer *God*

- the seed - *Word*

- the hard path *Devil take word*

- the shallow soil

- the thorns

- the fertile soil — *take it to heart*
  + bare fruit

How does this parable impact your own witnessing?

5. Give an example of something you could do that is perfectly fine for you but could offend another believer. Give at least two reasons why you should refrain from doing this rather than asking the other person to be less legalistic.

6. Why do you think Paul felt Timothy should be circumcised (Acts 16:3)? What does the phrase "in deference to the Jews" mean?

7. Timothy was from a mixed marriage (Jewish mother and Greek father). What message might Paul have been sending out by choosing someone like Timothy?

Part 5

The Church Expands to Macedonia and Greece
Acts 16:6–19:20

Did you know that God prepared the way for the Good News of Jesus to go out to the world long before Jesus was even born? God prepared the political, cultural, and technological conditions so the amazing things recorded by Luke in Acts would happen.

- *Politically* the Roman Empire controlled the Middle Eastern and Western world, creating unity and political stability. This unification and *Pax Romana* (the peace of Rome) made travel from region to region relatively easy.

- *Culturally* the Hellenistic Empire (*Hellenism* is another word for Greek culture) had spread throughout the civilized world due to the conquests of Alexander the Great. Because of this the common language of the world was Greek. Even in Rome, where Latin was the official language, most people spoke Greek.

- *Technologically* the Roman Empire was connected by a series of roads that were justly famous (no doubt you've heard the expression "all roads lead to Rome").

When the followers of Christ began to carry out His commission to tell people everywhere about Him, God had things ready. Those early missionaries could travel in a stable political environment along a well-developed transportation system and preach the message of Christ in a language everybody understood. Isn't God amazing!

Chapter 9

Paul's Second and Third Missionary Journeys

Acts 16:6–19:20

*W*hat's *A*head

- Paul's Second Missionary Journey (16:6-40)
- Thessalonica and Berea (17:1-15)
- Preaching in Athens (17:16-34)
- Ministering in Corinth and Ephesus (18:1-28)
- Paul's Third Missionary Journey (19:1-20)

*I*n some ways, the Holy Spirit is like a spiritual travel agent. On this journey called the Christian life, He maps out our itinerary, choosing the very best places and people He wants us to see and meet. Following His plans is always a good idea because He sees the big picture, He knows what's best, and He prepares the way. We're about to see the Holy Spirit in action as the Christian message expands once again into new regions and cities.

Paul's Second Missionary Journey (16:6-40)

Luke doesn't explain why God doesn't want Paul and Silas to go to Asia, but in hindsight we can see that the next step in their journey becomes a key turning point in the history of the church. Because of Paul's obedience, the Gospel went to the West and eventually to Europe. We may not always understand God's leading, but we don't have to. We just have to obey and take the next step, trusting God with the final result.

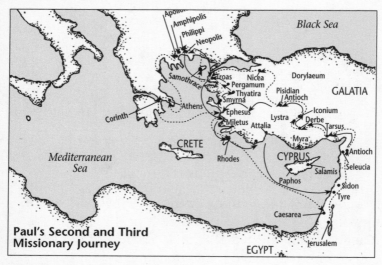

Paul's Second and Third Missionary Journey

Directed by God (16:6-10)

Notice in this passage that Luke makes reference to all three Persons in the Godhead:

- The *Holy Spirit* told them not to go to Asia (16:6).

- The *Spirit of Jesus* did not let them go to Bithynia (16:7).

- *God* called them to preach the Good News in Macedonia (16:10).

What a dynamic picture of the Trinity—God the Father, God the Son, and God the Holy Spirit—working together to direct His children. The Trinity can be a tough concept to get our minds around, yet it is foundational to the church and our Christian beliefs. As Christians, we are the *people of God*, belonging to the *body of Christ*, living in the *power of the Holy Spirit*.

ℒuke Joins the 𝒫arty

From the "we" in 16:10, we can see that Luke has joined the missionary team of Paul, Silas, and Timothy. Luke was from this area, and Troas may have been his hometown. Some scholars believe Luke ended up living in Philippi, the city the team visits next.

Lydia Believes (16:11-15)

The four missionaries sail across the Aegean Sea to Macedonia and the city of Philippi. Macedonia was the homeland of Alexander the Great, and Philippi was a Roman colony created by Caesar Augustus (the Roman emperor from 27 B.C. to A.D. 14) as a home for military veterans. Philippi has no synagogue, so the team goes to a place where people meet for prayer. There they encounter Lydia, a successful merchant who, like Cornelius, worships God but doesn't know Jesus. The Lord opens her heart (another indication of God's sovereignty in salvation), and she and her household are saved. Lydia invites Paul and his associates to be guests in her home, and so begins the church at Philippi, a place that gave Paul much joy (Philippians 1:3-5).

Paul and Silas Go to Jail (16:16-28)

Paul and Silas encounter a demon-possessed slave girl owned by some men who are profiting handsomely from her fortune-telling abilities. She follows the missionaries around, telling everyone the truth about their mission (see James 2:19). At first her ranting may have drawn attention to Paul and Silas (kind of like an annoying but effective publicity agent), but after a while she becomes a nuisance, so Paul casts out the demon in her.

This immediately reduces the slave girl's income potential to zero, which upsets her owners. Incensed, they drag Paul and Silas before the authorities and accuse them, not of casting out the demon but of being Jews. Claudius, the current Roman emperor (A.D. 41–54) had recently expelled the Jews from Rome, so Philippi was probably full of anti-Semitism. This may explain why Timothy, a half-Gentile, and Luke, a full-blooded Gentile, aren't thrown into jail along with Paul and Silas.

Another Jail Miracle—but Not a Jailbreak (16:29-34)

After city officials beat Paul and Silas and throw them into jail, the two missionaries organize a prayer and praise service with the other inmates. For the third time in Acts, God shows His power in the local hoosegow, but this time nobody leaves. This is a good thing for the jailer, who is about to take his life (he knows the penalty for allowing prisoners to escape). Paul stops him from killing himself, which prompts the jailer to ask the world's most important question: "What must I do to be saved?"

Perhaps the jailer had heard about the miracle of the slave girl. Maybe he heard the singing, praising, and preaching. He definitely felt the power of God as the earth shook. He was ready to receive Christ! And Paul was ready to explain the simple message of the Gospel:

> *Believe on the Lord Jesus and you will be saved, along with your entire household* (16:31).

That's all you need to do to be justified before God: Have faith alone in Christ alone.

A Violation of Rights (16:35-40)

The authorities order the jailer to release the two Jews, but Paul and Silas announce that they are Roman citizens whose rights have been violated on several counts. Why did they wait until *after* their beatings and incarceration to inform the city officials of their Roman citizenship? Clinton Arnold speculates that Paul and Silas were willing to suffer in order to set an example for the other believers who may not have a Roman citizenship to protect them.

> God's power plus our witness and the proclamation of the Word bring about salvation.

Thessalonica and Berea (17:1-15)

Paul and Silas travel 100 miles on the Roman road known as the Egnatian Way to Thessalonica, the capital of Macedonia and its biggest city.

Converts in Thessalonica (17:1-9)

Paul heads for the synagogue, and over a period of weeks he opens the Scriptures, explaining that the Messiah the Jews are looking for is the resurrected Jesus. This is tough for these Thessalonian Jews to accept because most Jews were expecting a political deliverer, not a suffering Savior. In addition to the "godly Greek men" (these are Gentiles who have turned from the Greek deities to the one true God), Luke points to "many important women" who also become converts. The mention of influential women here, as in Philippi, is no coincidence. God-fearing women outnumbered God-fearing men in the ancient Near East. Once again the Jewish leaders are jealous, inciting a mob to ransack the home of Jason, who is hosting Paul and Silas.

The Noble Bereans (17:10-15)

The atmosphere in Thessalonica must be a little too intense because Paul and Silas slip out at night and travel about 50 miles to Berea. We like the way the NIV describes the Jews in this city: "Now the Bereans were of more noble character than the Thessalonians" (17:11). The reason for this description is that these Jews examine the Scriptures to make sure the message Paul and Silas are delivering is true. The result of their honest search is that many people believe.

Be a Noble Believer!

We need to be people of noble character who search the Scriptures, not in a critical way just to prove somebody wrong, but in a responsible way to hold others accountable to the truth. Always compare the things you hear, whether from believers or unbelievers, with the Bible. Of course, that means you have to get to know the Bible, which is what you are doing in this study. Congratulations! You're on your way to nobility!

Preaching in Athens (17:16-34)

Some people from Thessalonica come to Berea and cause trouble for Paul, so he travels to Athens, where he waits for Timothy and Silas to join him. While in Athens, he does a little sightseeing.

Idols and Philosophers (17:16-21)

As Paul walks the streets of Athens, he's troubled by the great number of idols he sees. (Athens, like most Greek and Roman cities, was filled with temples, idols, and altars to the various gods and goddesses of mythology.) He notices one particular idol marked with the inscription "To an Unknown God." Paul uses this as a touch point for his debate in the Areopagus, a place where Stoic, Epicurean, and other philosophers meet to debate and discuss the latest ideas.

Paul Addresses the Philosophers (17:22-31)

Paul's message to the philosophers is more of a discourse than a sermon. It's a classic three-point talk:

- *Introduction: The Unknown God (17:22-23).* Paul compliments the philosophers for being "very religious," referring to the altar of the Unknown God, which they have been worshipping. Paul is not saying that they are already following the one true God without knowing His name. He's merely setting up the question everyone needs to answer: Who is God?

- *Main Point: The One True God (17:24-28).* Paul brilliantly and succinctly defines the one true God by describing His attributes and acts of creation. God is the source of life and breath, and He is personally involved with His created beings. God is transcendent—that is, He exists apart from His creation—but He desires a personal relationship with us.

- *Conclusion: Turn to God (17:29-31).* Though he doesn't mention Jesus by name, Paul clearly concludes his talk with the saving message of Christ. He tells the philosophers to "turn away from idols and turn to him" (17:30). For there is a day coming when all will be judged by the resurrected Christ (17:31).

The Philosophers Respond (17:32-34)

A few believe, but by and large the philosophers reject Paul's message. Many who read this passage today conclude that Paul's message failed because he watered it down for his Greek audience and never mentioned the name of Jesus. Clinton Arnold disagrees with this, saying, "Paul's entire message is thoroughly rooted in biblical worldview and not in Greek polytheistic, pantheistic, or dualistic worldview." The problem is more with the attitude of the Athenians than with Paul's method or message.

Ministering in Corinth and Ephesus (18:1-28)

In his letter to the church at Corinth, Paul writes that he first came to them "in weakness—timid and trembling" (1 Corinthians 2:3). He must be discouraged after his experience in Athens. Still, he trusts what God says: "My gracious favor is all you need. My power works best in your weakness" (2 Corinthians 12:9).

Corrupt Corinth

With a population of well over 100,000, Corinth was much larger and, as the provincial capital, more important than Athens. It also had a reputation for great immorality. A thousand "sacred" prostitutes filled the temple of the goddess Aphrodite. As a result of these cultural influences, the Corinthian church was plagued by immorality and corruption among some of its members. In his first letter to the Corinthian church, Paul deals with these issues.

Fellow Tentmakers (18:1-3)

In his letter to the church at Thessalonica, Paul writes about earning a living "so that our expenses would not be a burden to anyone there as we preached God's Good News among you" (1 Thessalonians 2:9). Paul's means of earning a living is tent making, a trade he learned while he was a rabbi in training. As soon as Paul arrives in Corinth, he probably looks for a local tent maker so he can earn some money. God leads him to Priscilla and Aquila, a godly couple who were kicked out of Rome when Claudius expelled the Jews. They form a close and lasting friendship with Paul and open their home and pocketbooks to the church.

Preaching Full-Time (18:4-23)

Timothy and Silas join Paul in Corinth, bringing with them a gift from the Philippian church (Philippians 4:15; 2 Corinthians 11:9). This enables Paul to devote all of his time to preaching, although his ministry in Corinth starts out a lot like the experience in Antioch of Pisidia: preaching, rejection, and shaking the dust from his robes. Paul could have again become discouraged, but God encourages him in a vision. After 18 months in Corinth, Paul completes his second missionary journey with trips to Ephesus, Caesarea, and Jerusalem before returning to his home base in Antioch.

Giving Apollos Some Guidance (18:24-28)

Apollos is a superstar. Blessed with a natural talent for public speaking, he wows the crowds in Ephesus with his "great enthusiasm and accuracy about Jesus." However, he lacks some knowledge about the Christian message. Specifically, he doesn't understand the significance of what God accomplished through the death and resurrection of Christ. Priscilla and Aquila notice and take the young evangelist under their wing, explaining "the way of God more accurately." The teachable Apollos responds and continues to preach with great power.

Paul's Third Missionary Journey (19:1-20)

Within a year Paul embarks on his third missionary journey, which would roughly follow the same pattern as his second journey. The main difference is that he decides to make Ephesus his base of operation. He ends up staying in this major business center (it was the capital of the province of Asia) for about three years, more than twice as long as he stayed anywhere else during his travels. While at Ephesus, Paul writes his first letter to the Corinthians.

Baptized in the Name of Jesus (19:1-7)

Paul meets 12 believers who, like Apollos (before he was enlightened by Priscilla and Aquila), are focusing on the teachings of John the Baptist. However, unlike

Apollos, who followed Christ, these disciples are stuck on John. Paul carefully explains to them that John's purpose was to point to Christ as the only one who can forgive sin. They believe and are baptized in the name of Jesus.

Two Years in a Lecture Hall (19:8-10)

After being partially rebuffed in the synagogue, Paul moves his ministry to a public lecture hall that was possibly rented and paid for by that faithful couple, Priscilla and Aquila. Tradition holds that Paul held lectures and had discussions about the claims of Christ from 11 A.M. to 4 P.M.—for two years! The result of this was astounding. Because of Paul's consistency and creative approach to spreading the Gospel, "people throughout the province of Asia—both Jews and Gentiles—heard the Lord's message."

*T*hink *O*utside the *B*ox

We need to constantly think about how to be creative in our witnessing efforts. Don't assume that people who need to hear the claims of Christ will always come to a church or a place where Christians regularly meet. Go into the public places—meeting halls, college campuses, convention centers, even homes—and deliver your Good News message in a way that will engage the culture. Like Paul, partner with local Christians with a heart for ministry who can underwrite the cost of such programs.

An Exorcism Backfires (19:11-20)

As the curtain comes down on part 5 of Acts, we see God doing some unusual miracles through Paul, and then we catch a glimpse of a traveling magic show featuring the seven sons of a priest. When these yahoos try to cast out a demon in the name of Jesus, the demon (who knows Jesus and Paul but doesn't know these charlatans) turns on them and beats them senseless. This frightening episode literally puts the fear of God into the citizens of Ephesus, many of whom routinely dabble in the occult. Even some of the Christians fess up that they haven't completely separated themselves from their wicked past.

Writing to the church at Ephesus years later, Paul gave glory to God for what happened: "Now he is far above any ruler or authority or power or leader or anything else in this world or in the world to come" (Ephesians 1:21).

So the message about the Lord spread widely and had a powerful effect (Acts 19:20).

◼ ◼ ◼

Study the Word

1. God prepared the world for the first coming of His Son to earth. Do you think God is getting the world ready for Christ's second coming? How?

    Yes through the resurrection

2. Luke doesn't tell us exactly how the Holy Spirit revealed His will to Paul. How does God reveal His will to you?

3. Read 1 Peter 4:12-19. How can you rejoice in your trials and suffering?

By knowing of our Salvation

4. List the qualities and characteristics of God the Father, God the Son, and God the Holy Spirit displayed in each of these passages:

• Romans 1:1-4

• Galatians 3:1-14

• Ephesians 1:3-14

5. What can you learn from the way Paul exercised his rights as a Roman citizen? Give an example of an injustice that Christians may face as they attempt to witness for Christ. What can we do in the face of such opposition?

6. Many people claim to know and even follow God, yet like the philosophers in Athens, they don't know the one true God. Using Paul's words in 17:22-31 as a guide, list three qualities about God that you could explain to someone who needs to know the truth.

   Dad is every where
   Promises

7. The town where you live may not have a temple filled with a thousand prostitutes, but what are some of the other cultural influences that can grab your attention? As a believer trying to live your life the way God wants you to live, what can you do to keep these negative influences from affecting you? What does being *in* the world but not *of* the world mean?

Part 6
Back to Jerusalem and
On to Rome
Acts 19:21–28:31

In part 5 of Acts we saw that ministering for Christ has its ups and downs. You encounter someone like Lydia, whose heart has been opened to receive God's Good News message, and you are filled with confidence and hope. But then you run into people like the Athenian philosophers, and discouragement and even doubt set in. When we are discouraged, we need to remember that in good times and bad, whether the message is welcomed or opposed, God is working through it all. He sees the big picture, and He has a plan to use us if we will just remain faithful to Him.

In this final part of Acts, we're going to see more opposition and persecution, but we're also going to see Paul proclaiming the Gospel before governors and kings, just as Christ commissioned him to do (9:15). We don't know how far or how high God wants to take us as we witness for Him. We just know He has promised to be with us wherever we go.

Chapter 10

Paul Travels to Jerusalem

Acts 19:21–21:14

*W*hat's *A*head

- ☐ Trouble in Ephesus (19:21-41)

- ☐ Paul Does a Lot of Talking (20:1-38)

- ☐ On to Jerusalem (21:1-14)

*A*t this point in Paul's missionary career, he believes that his work in this part of the empire is nearing completion (Romans 15:23). His desire now is to return to Jerusalem and then go to Rome, a city he has never seen. Of course, he can't hop a nonstop boat from Ephesus to Jerusalem. He has many places and people to visit first.

Trouble in Ephesus (19:21-41)

Before he can leave, Paul must deal with some issues in Ephesus.

Paul Makes Plans (19:21-22)

Paul's intention to visit Jerusalem is partly motivated by his desire to personally take a collection from the

Gentile churches in Macedonia, Achaia (Greece), and Asia, who want to support the poorer church in Jerusalem (2 Corinthians 9:1-10). Consequently, the movement in Acts in this chapter is going to take Paul from Ephesus to Macedonia, Corinth, Troas, and Miletus before he arrives in Jerusalem.

Should You Let the Spirit Lead You or Should You Make Your Own Decision?

Regarding Paul's plans to travel to Jerusalem, the NLT translates 19:21 like this: "Afterward Paul felt impelled by the Holy Spirit...." However, the NIV translates the same verse this way: "After all this had happened, Paul decided...." So which is it? Was Paul *led* by the Holy Spirit to do what he did, or did he *decide* on his own to go? Have you ever wondered about that in your own life? You know you need to do something, so do you wait for the Holy Spirit to lead you, or do you use your own best judgment to make a decision? You may sometimes feel God's clear direction, but you may also be in situations where you need to make a decision but don't feel God's definite direction either way. What should you do?

Reading 19:21 this way may help: "Paul decided by the direction of the Spirit...." What that means is that when we are living in the power of the Holy Spirit as a natural and ongoing part of our lives, we don't always have to wait for overt signals. We can use our own Spirit-filled judgment to make decisions that will work for our good and the benefit of others while giving glory to God.

Persecution Motivated by Money (19:23-41)

One of the big attractions in Ephesus for both the locals and the tourists was its great Temple of Artemis, the Greek goddess of fertility (the Roman counterpart to Artemis was Diana). The people of Ephesus were crazy about Artemis, so they constructed a temple with 127 majestic columns that was four times larger than the Greek Parthenon in Athens. The Temple of Artemis was one of the Seven Wonders of the Ancient World.

Tourists and pilgrims alike flocked to Ephesus to take in the culture and see the temple. The souvenir business in Ephesus was booming, and the most popular items were replicas of the Temple of Artemis and shrines to the goddess herself made out of silver. In fact, the economy of Ephesus was largely driven by the tourist trade and especially by the sale of these temple souvenirs.

As the church in Ephesus grew and people believed in Jesus rather than Artemis, sales for the silver souvenirs began to shrink. The leader of the silversmiths in Ephesus was a man named Demetrius, who blamed Paul and the Christians for the significant loss of business. At a meeting of the Ephesus Chamber of Commerce, Demetrius said, "As you have seen and heard, this man Paul has persuaded many people that handmade gods aren't gods at all. And this is happening not only here in Ephesus but throughout the entire province!" (19:26). A riot nearly breaks out, all because those pesky Christians and their message of forgiveness in Christ is persuading the Ephesians to follow the one true God rather than their fake silver god.

Just as Gamaliel prevented an ugly scene in Jerusalem from getting worse by appealing to God's sovereignty (5:33-39), the mayor of Ephesus steps in and prevents a riot or something worse from happening in his city by appealing to the sovereignty of Rome. Because an uprising in any form in the Roman Empire would cause the local leader to lose his job, this guy is protecting the Christians in order to preserve his own hide.

Paul Does a Lot of Talking (20:1-38)

With the trouble in Ephesus subsided, Paul rounds up the believers and gives them a pep talk. He then continues with his travel plans to Jerusalem.

Back to Corinth and Troas (20:1-6)

Paul makes some stops in Macedonia (probably Philippi), where he writes his second letter to the Corinthians. He then heads down to Greece, where he spends three months and writes his letter to the church in Rome. Following this little break, Paul returns to Philippi rather than going to Jerusalem by way of Syria, where some Jews are plotting to kill him. After Passover, Luke joins Paul, and together they sail to Troas.

The Inspiration of the Holy Spirit— Then and Now

Can you imagine writing such a lofty letter as Romans in three months? Paul was very smart and a gifted communicator, but he could never have written Romans without the inspiration of the Holy Spirit (2 Timothy 3:16). And think about this. The same Holy Spirit who inspired Luke to write Acts, who inspired Paul to write his letters, and who inspired all of the other 38 authors to write the rest of the Bible—that same Holy Spirit will guide you into the truth of Scripture as you read it (John 16:13). *1550*

Falling Asleep in Church (20:7-12)
1595

Picture this scene: The believers in Troas are packed into a third-story room to hear Paul, their teacher and friend, encourage them and share from God's Word. Paul will be leaving the next day and may never return, so this is no ordinary meeting. At midnight, Paul is still talking. The flickering lamps (think torches) are sucking oxygen out of the already hot room. Several of those gathered are getting drowsy, including a young man by the name of Eutychus, who is sitting on the windowsill and falls into a deep sleep. Suddenly he falls head over heels out the window.

Someone shouts to the group that the poor lad has fallen to his death. Paul rushes down, bends over the lifeless body, and holds it in his arms. Instantly Eutychus wakes up and everyone goes back upstairs to share the Lord's Supper together. Paul continues to teach until dawn.

If you were to reach a conclusion about this story, what would it be?

- a warning against falling asleep in church

- a warning against preachers who go on too long

Actually, it's neither (although we have to admit both options are tempting). The correct conclusion is the one Richard Longenecker makes: "It was an evening of great significance for the church at Troas: Paul had taught them, they had fellowship in the Lord's Supper, and they had witnessed a dramatic sign of God's presence and power."

A Message for the Ephesian Elders (20:13-38) 1595

Paul is anxious to get to Jerusalem for Pentecost, but he still takes time to meet with the Ephesian elders. Paul isn't safe in Ephesus, so the elders come to Miletus, where Paul is staying. He gives them a farewell message that contains several key points that are a model for us as we serve the Lord:

- Paul has faithfully served the Lord, even in danger and other difficulties (20:18-19).

- His message has focused on the necessity of turning away from sin and turning to God (20:20-21).

- Telling others the Good News of God's wonderful kindness and love in Christ has given his life meaning (20:22-24).

- He has obeyed God completely (20:25-27).

After telling the elders about his philosophy of ministry, Paul gives them some words of instruction:

- Those who lead God's people have a responsibility to care for them and feed them (20:28).

- Beware of false teachers who will come into your group (20:29).

- Some people among you will "distort the truth in order to draw a following" (20:30).

Paul isn't bragging here. He just knows that in the three years he stayed in Ephesus, he lived a life worth emulating.

- He cared for them day and night, shedding many tears.

- He never once wanted someone else's money or property.

- He worked to pay his own way.

- He paid for the needs of others.

- He served as an example by serving the poor.

1596

On to Jerusalem (21:1-14)

Following God's will isn't always a matter of choosing between what's bad and what's good. If you're living in the power of the Holy Spirit, that's an easy decision. The more difficult choice to make is between what's good and what's better, or between what's better and what's best. That's the kind of decision Paul is facing in this passage. He is determined to go to Jerusalem, even though he will likely be imprisoned once he sets foot in the city. His friends are convinced he should stay with them and play it safe. For Paul, going on to Jerusalem, where he believes God is calling him, would be a better decision—if not the best.

To make the situation even more difficult, nearly everywhere Paul goes, some believers are prophesying "through the Holy Spirit" that he should not go to Jerusalem. The prophet Agabus, who predicted the famine in Jerusalem 15 years earlier (11:27-29), gives a dramatic object lesson to show Paul what will happen if he goes. Even Luke joins in and begs Paul not to go (21:12).

Have you ever felt this kind of pressure? In your heart you are convinced that God wants you to do something. Yet other well-meaning people don't see it that way. No doubt they have your welfare in mind. Maybe they are concerned for your safety. So they tell you they have prayed about it and feel you should change your mind. What should you do?

When we see Paul going against everyone's advice, we need to read between the lines. He wasn't simply discounting the wise counsel of others. Rather, he was doing what he knew God wanted him to do, regardless of the danger. In fact, *danger* is the key issue here. Agabus doesn't prophesy that Paul shouldn't go, but that Paul will be arrested and turned over to the Romans if he does. As for the prophecies of the believers in Tyre, the Holy Spirit may have been telling them about the danger and nothing more. Out of good intentions, they may have wrongly interpreted the Spirit's leading to mean that Paul shouldn't go.

To put it another way, Paul knows that his friends are trying to talk him out of going because they fear for his safety. No one is seriously objecting to the great need in Jerusalem, and no one thinks Paul is incapable of handling any persecution he might face. In the end, Paul's resolve to suffer willingly for Christ overrides any concern for his well-being. He's not foolish, but faithful. Paul is being obedient, not obstinate. He's choosing the best over the better.

Following Your Heart by Following the Lord

A time may come when you have to go against the grain by following what you know to be God's will for your life. Like Paul, you need to show respect to those who love and care for you. And you need to live your life in such a way that others will say of you, as they did of Paul, "The will of the Lord be done."

■ ■ ■

Study the Word

1. Give an example of a time when you were clearly directed by the Holy Spirit to do something. What happened and what was the result? Now give an example of a time when you made a decision using your best Spirit-filled judgment. What happened and what was the result?

2. We don't have temples to Greek gods and goddesses in our communities, but what "shrines" and "temples" do we have that occupy our attention, time, and money? What happens when Christ comes in and redirects the desire we once had to "worship" at these places?

3. One of the most important ways the Holy Spirit helps us is by guiding us to the truth of Scripture (John 16:13). This probably doesn't mean we should sit back and wait for the Holy Spirit to download information into our brains. What practical steps can we take to cooperate with the Holy Spirit's teaching process?

4. Pastor Kent Hughes writes that he has great sympathy for people who fall asleep in church. What bothers him are people whose bodies are awake but whose souls are asleep. Their eyes may be open, but their minds have wandered off, and their hearts are far from God. What can you do to keep your soul from falling asleep, in church or anywhere else?

5. When Paul speaks to the Ephesian elders, he is basically giving his personal testimony. Evaluate your own spiritual life in the terms Paul used in his testimony.

   • Have you faithfully served the Lord?

   • What has been your message?

   • What has given your life meaning?

   • Have you obeyed God completely?

6. Describe the last time you had to choose between what's better and what's best. What was the outcome?

Chapter 11

Drama in Jerusalem

Acts 21:15–23:22

*W*hat's *A*head

- ☐ Conflict in Jerusalem (21:15-36)

- ☐ Paul Defends Himself (21:37–22:29)

- ☐ Before the High Council (22:30–23:22)

*I*t's lonely at the top. You've probably heard that expression, and you may have experienced it. The apostle Paul knew firsthand what it meant. Although Paul never considered himself to be the "top dog" of the early church, he was recognized as a very influential person. As a result, people were constantly criticizing him. As we saw in the last chapter, even his most faithful supporters sometimes questioned his motives and actions. But that's the way it is with leadership. If you are setting yourself apart from the pack by doing what God wants you to do, people will criticize you, and you will certainly meet with opposition. Yet you still have to work with the people God puts in your life, including your critics and enemies.

How to Handle Criticism

When people criticize and oppose you, the tendency is to either fight back or go it alone. Paul didn't react that way. Whenever possible, he accommodated those who disagreed with him if he could advance the cause of Christ and preserve the unity of the body. At the same time, if he had the opportunity to help others understand his position, he argued persuasively. Take the case of Luke. He was initially opposed to Paul's going to Jerusalem (21:12), but after seeing how determined Paul was to follow God's will, he went with Paul (21:15) and stuck with him. In a letter written to Timothy from prison, Paul said, "Only Luke is with me" (2 Timothy 4:11).

Conflict in Jerusalem (21:15-36)

Before we look at what Paul does to preserve the unity with the Jerusalem church, let's examine Paul's report to James and the elders. Luke writes, "After greetings were exchanged, Paul gave a detailed account of the things God had accomplished among the Gentiles through his ministry" (21:19). Notice that Paul gives credit where credit is due. Even though Paul is the one who has been working hard to spread the Gospel, enduring criticism from his friends and persecution from his enemies, he says God has accomplished it all.

What a critical principle for us! We may be involved in great things for God. We may even lead a ministry where others look to us for spiritual direction. But we must never think that we are the ones accomplishing things for God. Anything done for the Lord and through the Lord is accomplished by the Lord. If anything, we need to take the position of John the Baptist, who said,

"He must become greater and greater, and I must become less and less" (John 3:30).

Preserving the Unity (21:15-26)

At the conclusion of Paul's report, the elders praise God. But they've also got some criticism for Paul. They are glad that all these Gentiles are being saved, but a bunch of Jews are getting saved in Jerusalem too. And these Jewish believers think Paul is teaching the Jews living in Gentile lands to disregard the Mosaic Law. This criticism is unwarranted of course, but Paul still has to deal with it. In order to preserve the unity in the church, he agrees to their suggestion involving four men who have been following a Nazirite vow. (Paul once took a Nazirite vow—see Acts 18:18. And Samson was dedicated to God as a Nazirite—see Judges 13:7. To read more about what this vow involved, see Numbers 6.)

These four men are about to end their vow by sacrificing animals and cutting their hair. In order to show his support of the Jewish Christians and to dispel rumors that he is against the Mosaic Law, the elders of the church ask Paul to participate in the ceremony by paying for it (a sign of piety) and by going through a purification ritual of his own.

A Mob Tries to Kill Paul (21:27-36)

Just as he is completing his purification ritual, Paul is attacked by a mob of unbelieving Jews who falsely accuse him of bringing a Gentile into the Temple. This is a violation punishable by death, not only for the Gentile intruder but also for the Jew responsible for the defilement. If the Roman commander doesn't intervene and arrest Paul, the mob is probably going to kill Paul.

Paul Takes the High Road

Once again Paul takes the high road in this matter with the Jerusalem Christians and the law. We see how serious he was about preserving the unity of the church. Rather than exercising his rights to be free from the law, he respects the traditions of his Jewish brothers and sisters. Paul knows that keeping or not keeping these traditions isn't the issue. In his letter to the Corinthian church, he says, "It's true that we can't win approval by what we eat. We don't miss out on anything if we don't eat it, and we don't gain anything if we do" (1 Corinthians 8:8). But he also doesn't want to be a stumbling block to other believers: "But you must be careful with this freedom of yours. Do not cause a brother or sister with a weaker conscience to stumble" (1 Corinthians 8:9).

Put yourself in Paul's place. He has just returned from ministering to Gentiles, who eagerly accepted the message of salvation. Now the Jews of Jerusalem are trying to kill him for bringing the same message. "In this rejection of the Christian message," writes Larkin, "we see the last major spiritual and geographic turning point in Acts." Once he leaves Jerusalem, Paul will never come back. Spiritually, the rejection symbolizes Israel's failure to fulfill its divinely intended mission as a "light to the Gentiles" (Isaiah 49:6). Larkin writes: "By shutting out the messenger and the message of salvation, Paul's opponents have sealed the city's doom." Paul will make one more effort to reason with the crowd by explaining his mission, but the damage has been done. This reminds us of what Jesus said about His beloved city:

> O Jerusalem, Jerusalem, the city that kills the
> prophets and stones God's messengers! How often
> I have wanted to gather your children together as

a hen protects her chicks beneath her wings, but you wouldn't let me. And now look, your house is left to you empty. And you will never see me again until you say, "Bless the one who comes in the name of the Lord!" (Luke 13:34-35).

Paul Defends Himself (21:37–22:29)

As he is being led away, Paul asks the Roman commander permission to address the crowd. He grants it, and Paul motions for the mob to calm down. They get even quieter when he begins talking to them in their own language. Showing respect to the "brothers and esteemed fathers," he tells the religious leaders that he was once one of them—a zealous Pharisee who honored God in all he did. Paul also makes clear that he wants to offer a robust defense against the charges against him. His defense has four parts.

- *Paul was once a persecutor* (22:4-5). He wants the audience to be aware of his zeal for God, a quality the religious leaders would admire.

- *His persecution was against Jesus* (22:6-11). Paul's zeal for God was misdirected. In fact, he wasn't persecuting Christians, but Christ.

- *He must tell the whole world what he has seen and heard* (22:12-16). Ananias, a devout and respected Jew, told Paul that he had been chosen by "the God of our ancestors" to take the message of "the Righteous One" to the whole world. This was a clear reference to the Law (Exodus 3:13) and the prophets (Zechariah 9:9).

- *Paul must take the message to the Gentiles* (22:17-21).
  God is the one who commanded Paul to take the
  message of Christ to the Gentiles. Still, Paul is a
  faithful Jew.

Claiming Roman Citizenship (22:24-29)

Paul's defense falls on deaf ears, so the commander
decides to have Paul flogged. He doesn't know why the
crowd is so angry with Paul, so he is hoping that physical punishment will force Paul to confess to his crime.

More than a Beating

Paul has been beaten by the Jews and the Romans many times
before, but this punishment was going to be different. Paul
was about to be flogged—or *scourged*—a brutal procedure
involving a whip of thongs studded with pieces of bone or
metal. The victim was tied to a pillar while the whip is repeat-
edly applied, tearing chunks of flesh from his back, resulting in
serious physical damage and sometimes death. Jesus was
scourged before His crucifixion (John 19:1).

Paul isn't afraid of another beating, but he probably
knows that this one could kill him. He also knows that a
Roman citizen cannot be punished until he has been
proven guilty of a crime, so Paul decides to invoke his
Roman citizenship. This new information rattles the
commander, who quickly stops the "interrogation."
Once again we see Paul using his earthly rights to help
his heavenly cause. Paul advises that we obey the
authorities, who are sent by God to help us (Romans
13:1-5). But if the authorities are treating us or others
unjustly, we have the right and the responsibility to
appeal to the rule of law.

Before the High Council (22:30–23:22)

Paul is released from his chains, but he's still a prisoner, and he will remain a prisoner for the rest of Acts. Frustrated that he still doesn't know what Paul has done wrong, the commander turns Paul over to an emergency session of the high council, hoping that the Jewish leaders will be able to sort things out.

$\mathscr{P}$harisees and $\mathscr{S}$adducees

The two main Jewish religious groups were the Pharisees and Sadducees. The Pharisees were very legalistic, but they believed in the resurrection for all human beings after death. The Sadducees did not believe in the immortality of the soul and the resurrection of the dead.

1599

Paul Divides the Council (22:30–23:11)

Ananias, who served as the high priest from A.D. 47–59, was described by the Jewish historian Josephus as a greedy, violent, hot-tempered man. As soon as Paul opens his mouth and says he is not aware of any wrongdoing, Ananias orders someone to smack him in the mouth. This abrupt move is humiliating and against the protocol of law, causing Paul to react in anger. In one sense we enjoy seeing that Paul is no wimp, but in another sense Paul's response is a little out of character. When Paul realizes that he's talking to the high priest, he apologizes. He knows what the Scriptures say about respecting those who rule over you. (J. Vernon McGee speculates that Paul's poor eyesight or even an eye disease was the reason Paul didn't recognize Ananias in the first place.)

Paul then brings up a topic—the resurrection of the dead—that divides the council. When you first read these verses, Paul appears to be doing this in order to start a fight between the Pharisees and the Sadducees. This would seem like a pretty effective tactic, but Paul is probably bringing up the resurrection, especially the resurrection of Jesus, because it's the central fact of Christianity and its true hope. This is why Paul is preaching. This is why Paul is on trial. If Jesus had not risen from the dead, Paul would not have met Jesus on the road to Damascus, and he would not have dedicated himself to spreading the Good News message that anyone who believes in Jesus will also be raised from the dead and have eternal life.

Without the Resurrection, We Are Without Hope

In his first letter to the Corinthians, Paul made it very clear that the resurrection is the central fact and hope of Christianity. "For if there is no resurrection of the dead, then Christ has not been raised either. And if Christ was not raised, then all our preaching is useless, and your trust in God is useless....And if we have hope in Christ only for this life, then we are the most miserable people in the world" (1 Corinthians 15:13-14,19). Paul would not have said this unless he knew that the resurrection was a fact.

The argument between the two groups gets so intense that the commander has to step in and protect Paul. That night in prison, God speaks to Paul, giving him both encouragement and instruction. God's will for Paul is that he goes to Rome.

16 00

A Plan to Kill Paul (23:12-22)

Once again we see God's direct hand of providence in the life of Paul. A group of more than 40 Jews has vowed to kill Paul, but they need the involvement of the high council. Paul's nephew hears of the plot and goes to the fortress where Paul is being kept. He shares the news with Paul, who in turn asks a centurion to take his nephew to the commander. Not only does the commander see the nephew, but he does so in private and agrees to keep the matter confidential.

God has a purpose and a plan for Paul because He has a purpose and a plan for His saving message. He will involve as many people as He needs—in this case a courageous nephew, a determined apostle, a willing centurion, and a thoughtful commander—to accomplish His purposes.

What about you? Have you seen God work in your life? Has He used other people to intervene in your life so that His message can go out? If not, then perhaps you are not involved in God's work. But if you've seen God's hand directing your life through people and circumstances, then you are where God wants you to be.

◼ ◼ ◼

Study the Word

1. What does it mean to be loyal to someone? What's the difference between a friend who "sticks closer than a brother" (Proverbs 18:24) and a fair-weather friend?

2. What happens when we think we are accomplishing things for God? How do you find the balance between confidence in your abilities and dependence on God?

3. Sometimes disagreements in churches can become so serious that you have no choice but to leave. But what if God calls you to stay in order to be an "agent of renewal"? List some of the ways God could use you to bring about positive change in a church with problems.

4. According to William Larkin, our freedom in Christ needs to be directed to two higher purposes: (1) to advance the Good News message of Christ, and (2) to promote the unity of the body. What happens when we don't use our freedom to accomplish these two goals?

5. Can people shut out the message of salvation so often that they seal their own doom? Why or why not?

6. Paul admitted he was wrong to talk back to Ananias. What does this tell you about Paul's character? Respond to this quote from Lloyd Ogilvie: "It's not our mistakes that do us in; it's our pride that keeps us from admitting them."

Chapter 12

Before Governors and a King

Acts 23:23–26:32

What's Ahead

When we think of "defending the faith," we usually think in terms of answering the questions posed by seekers and skeptics. But sometimes we may need to explain our Christian hope (1 Peter 3:15) to those in authority over us. That's what Paul gets the opportunity to do. On his way to Rome, the place God said he was going, Paul is about to stand before governors and a king, giving a defense of his faith in Christ.

In our culture, only a few people will be called before governors and presidents to explain their faith in Christ, but many of us may have the opportunity to witness to local authorities. Whether we stand before a school board to logically explain why the Creator of the universe deserves equal time with Darwin in science class, or we appear before the city council to argue in favor of religious freedom, we need to be prepared to give an answer to the hope that's in us. That's what Paul did. Let's learn from this master of both mind and character.

Paul Appears Before Governor Felix (23:23–24:27)

Claudius Lysias, the Roman commander who first arrested and then protected Paul, arranges for his prisoner to be transferred to Caesarea, the center of the Roman government for Judea. Since he can't find any reason to imprison or execute Paul, he is sending Paul to Governor Felix for trial.

Transported to Caesarea (23:23-35)

You might be wondering why Lysias needs 470 soldiers to transport one beaten-down prisoner with poor eyesight from Jerusalem to Caesarea, a trip of 60 miles. There are two reasons. First, the tensions between Jews and Romans are at an all-time high. Second, Lysias knows about the plot involving at least 40 Jews who want to kill Paul, and there may be more. He doesn't want to take any chances of failing to protect a Roman citizen.

The commander explains everything in a letter to Felix, who has been governor of Judea for five years. Felix is an interesting character. He's a former slave who is the first freedman in history to become the governor of a Roman province. Felix is politically savvy (his wife, Drusilla, is the daughter of Herod Agrippa I) and not above hiring hit men to take out his closest associates if he thinks they might betray him. Felix is a ruthless leader known for executing many Jewish zealots by crucifixion.

The Charges Against Paul (24:1-9)

Picture this: You've got the highest-ranking official in the province presiding over a trial in the capital city. The plaintiff is the Jewish high council, led by Ananias, the highest-ranking official in the Jewish nation. The defendant is Paul, a Christian missionary who has been accused of subversion against the state. The plaintiff has hired a high-priced, smooth-talking lawyer by the name of Tertullus. Paul has waived his rights to an attorney and has decided to represent himself. If this trial were being held today, every television channel would be covering it, and the political talk shows would be discussing it endlessly.

Tertullus' opening statement is classic. First he butters up Felix so much that even Felix is probably rolling his eyes. Then the crafty lawyer lays out the charges against Paul. Notice how politically charged the wording is. And watch how he doesn't tell the whole truth.

- *Paul has always been a troublemaker.* Tertullus implies that Paul is like a pestilence that has spread throughout the empire against the Roman government.

- *Paul is the leader of the Nazarene sect.* Tertullus is trying to establish that Christianity is not part of the Jewish religion. This is because the Roman government permits Judaism to operate as a legal religion but will not tolerate any new religions.

- *Paul is a defiler of the Temple.* Even this charge has political overtones. The Romans had given the Jews permission to execute any Gentile who passed the Temple barrier. Tertullus wants Felix to believe that

Paul broke this law by bringing a Gentile into the Temple—a bald-faced lie.

Paul Gives His Defense (24:10-21)

Paul shows respect to Felix, but he doesn't butter him up like Tertullus did. Paul uses three lines of defense:

- *Paul is a faithful Jew.* Paul explains that the only difference between his faith and Judaism is that his faith sees the hope of Judaism fulfilled in Jesus of Nazareth. He shows that his hope is in God, as is the Jewish leaders'. And like them (with the exception of the Sadducees), Paul believes in the resurrection for all people, just as the prophets foretold (Daniel 12:2). Therefore, far from being a new religion, Christianity is merely an outgrowth of Judaism and the Old Testament.

- *Paul's accusers aren't present.* The Asian Jews who first accused Paul aren't even at the trial to substantiate their charges. Because Roman law frowned upon accusers who couldn't personally back up their charges, this greatly damages the high council's case.

- *Paul has a clean record and a clean conscience.* Paul stands before Felix and God with a clear conscience because he has lived a blameless life.

When all is said and done, the only thing the Jews can charge Paul with is believing in the resurrection of the dead, something that clearly isn't a crime.

$\mathcal{A}$re $\mathcal{W}$e $\mathcal{B}$lameless?

On three different occasions when he must defend himself against religious and political authorities, Paul says that he has lived a blameless life. He has kept his conscience clear before both God and man. This record of integrity is an important part of his witness, and it should be a part of ours as well. When we compromise our integrity in any way, people have reason to doubt our commitment to Christ and the Christian message. We should be able not only to outthink our opponents but to outlive them as well. Ajith Fernando writes, "The force of blameless lives has been powerful in defending Christianity against attacks from outside in every age."

Felix Ponders Paul's Message (24:22-27)

Felix doesn't find enough evidence to convict Paul, so he adjourns the case until Lysias can testify. This appears to be a stall tactic because we don't know if Lysias ever comes to Caesarea, but we do know that two years pass without a decision from Felix. Being the politician that he is, Felix keeps Paul in custody to placate the Jews. During this time, Felix and his wife have some conversations with Paul. Luke says Felix is familiar with the Way, but we don't know how deep that knowledge goes. From Luke's account we do know that Paul gives Felix enough information to convict the governor—so much so that he sends Paul away.

Paul Appears Before Governor Festus (25:1-22)

Two years after Paul's trial, the higher-ups in Rome recall Felix from his position because of the inept way he handled a flare-up of violence between Jews and Greeks in Caesarea. His replacement is Festus, a Roman with much more integrity than his predecessor.

Why the Rich and Powerful Have Difficulty Turning to Christ

Felix had every reason to become terrified when Paul told him about righteousness, self-control, and the judgment to come. His life was characterized by immorality, and his administration was marked by injustice. Besides, he was a rich and powerful man, which made surrendering his life to Christ even tougher. Jesus once said that entering God's Kingdom was extremely difficult for the rich (Matthew 19:24). If we use Felix as an example, we can see several reasons why this is the case. First, they can hide their insecurities behind their positions. This is what Felix did. He simply sent Paul away. Second, they are often controlled by greed. As rich as he was, Felix was hoping for a bribe from Paul. Third, the rich and powerful usually want to please as many people as possible. When your goal is to please everybody, you probably will have a hard time pleasing God.

Paul Appeals to Caesar (25:1-12)

Just three days after taking office, Festus travels to Jerusalem to hear from the Jewish leaders. They know they can't win in court, so they request a change of venue from Caesarea to Jerusalem (of course, this is simply a way to set up an ambush). Festus wisely keeps the case in Caesarea, where the trial resumes. It's the same old story of unproven accusations that Paul denies. Thinking that he's doing the Jews a favor, Festus offers to preside over a trial in Jerusalem, but Paul is adamant. As a Roman citizen, he has the right to have his case heard in Rome by Emperor Nero himself. Seeing that his trial is going nowhere, knowing that the Jews want to kill him, and wanting to get to Rome, Paul exercises that right.

Festus Confers with King Agrippa (25:13-22)

Enter King Agrippa II, the son of Agrippa I, who executed James and imprisoned Peter 15 years earlier. Agrippa II, who rules territories northeast of Palestine, drops in on Festus to pay his respects to the recently appointed governor. Festus must be delighted, for he has the opportunity to consult with a ruler who has experience in Jewish affairs, even though Agrippa's jurisdiction does not include Judea. Agrippa asks to meet with Paul, and Festus agrees. Paul is about to fulfill the commission Jesus gave to him on the road to Damascus (9:15). But he is not going in alone. Here is what Jesus told His disciples when He first sent them out:

> And you must stand trial before governors and kings because you are my followers. This will be your opportunity to tell them about me—yes, to witness to the world. When you are arrested, don't worry about what to say in your defense, because you will be given the right words at the right time. For it won't be you doing the talking —it will be the Spirit of your Father speaking through you (Matthew 18:18-20).

The Holy Spirit Will Speak Through You

Here's another huge benefit of having the power of the Holy Spirit in your life. When you talk about the Lord to your non-Christian friends, your coworkers, your unsaved family members, or even those strangers God sends your way, the Holy Spirit will give you the right words at the right time. And should you be asked to speak to those in authority for whatever reason, have confidence that the Holy Spirit will speak through you.

Paul Appears Before King Agrippa (25:23–26:32)

This is a dramatic scene. The king and his entourage enter the auditorium with "great pomp." Waiting to receive them are the top military and city officials.

Festus Needs Help (25:23-27)

Festus is in a bit of a quandary. Roman law requires that he must write a report, including a summary of the case and the charges, before sending Paul to Rome for his appeal, and so far he can't come up with any charges. Festus is hoping that Agrippa can help him. Paul walks into the great hall, a humble, ragged figure in chains, standing before the most powerful rulers in Palestine. Yet in this man is the Spirit of the living God, maker of heaven and earth. All of the power and all of the kings of this world are no match for the One who reigns in glory and majesty!

Paul Tells His Story (26:1-23)

This will be the third time Luke has recorded the story of Paul's conversion (see also 9:1-30 and 22:3-21). As before, Luke gives us a summary of Paul's rather lengthy address. Because this is not a trial, Paul is explaining his beliefs more than he is defending his actions. As always, Paul knows how to adapt to his audience. He is aware that Agrippa, being a Jew himself, knows the Jewish "customs and controversies."

Paul tells Agrippa about the hope of the resurrection God promised to their ancestors. This is the issue at hand, and it is also the central fact of Christianity. If Christ has not been raised, then our faith is in vain. But Christ did rise, and Paul is an eyewitness, having met Jesus of Nazareth on the road to Damascus. Notice that Luke gives more details of Paul's encounter with Jesus here than in either of his other two testimonies. Acts 26:18 in particular is highly significant because it summarizes what God does for people when He saves them:

- He opens their eyes so they may turn from darkness to light (Ephesians 5:8).

- He frees them from Satan's power (Hebrews 2:14).

- He forgives their sins (Acts 2:38).

- He sets them apart by virtue of their faith in Him (1 Peter 2:9).

How could Paul disobey such a vision from heaven? Paul closes his remarks by stating once again that he is merely teaching "what the prophets and Moses said would happen—that the Messiah would suffer and be the first to rise from the dead as a light to Jews and Gentiles alike" (26:22-23).

Agrippa Responds (26:24-32)

Festus has heard enough, so he interrupts Paul and calls him a lunatic. Being a Roman, Festus can't relate to all this talk about the resurrection. According to Clinton Arnold, Romans believed the afterlife was a time when a person would finally be free from "the bondage of material existence." Paul immediately denies the label of insanity and appeals to Agrippa as one who would know what the prophets said. Of course, Agrippa can't admit to anything in front of this great assembly, so he answers Paul with a question of his own: "Do you think you can make me a Christian so quickly?" (26:28).

Paul responds in a way that shows his deep love for people. Oh, that we would care for the lost as much as Paul did. Can't you see Paul gesturing to the whole crowd—the king, the governor, the military commanders, the civic leaders, and everyone else—as he says in effect, "I pray that you would all become Christians!" May we pray for those who are without Christ and without hope with as much love and compassion as Paul had!

◼ ◼ ◼

Study the Word

1. Under what circumstances in our day must believers defend Christianity before the state? What is the most effective way of doing this? Who is best qualified to make an effective defense?

2. Tertullus used a series of half-truths to accuse Paul. What can you learn from Paul's defense that could help you answer someone who uses half-truths and distortions to criticize you and your faith?

3. Why is integrity such an important part of our witness? How does a breach in your integrity give people a reason to doubt you, or even worse, to doubt Christianity?

4. Describe a time when the Holy Spirit spoke through you as you talked to another person or group of people.

5. Why is accepting the resurrection of Christ as a fact so difficult for some people? List three things you would tell someone who asked you why you believe in the resurrection.

6. Despite Paul's stirring and eloquent testimony in front of Festus, Agrippa, and the rest, no one believed that day (at least none that we know about). What's the best thing to do when your message falls on deaf ears?

7. One of Luke's purposes in writing Acts was to show that Christianity is not a dangerous and subversive religion. Has he succeeded in getting his point across? How?

Chapter 13

The Journey to Rome

Acts 27–28

What's Ahead

☐ Sailing into a Storm (27:1-26)

☐ Shipwrecked on Malta (27:27–28:10)

☐ Rome At Last (28:11-31)

*A*fter the courtroom dramas, where Paul testified before governors and a king, you would think that a trip to Rome would be a snap. Board a ship, do a little sightseeing in the Mediterranean, and arrive safely in Italy all tanned and rested. Not so fast there, sailor! What human authorities have not been able to do, natural forces will now attempt: stopping God's plan to have Paul preach the Good News in Rome (23:11). As we come to the end of Acts, we're going to see nature's fury unleashed on Paul and his companions as they set sail.

Now, we're not saying that nature has a will that can oppose God, but we do know that because of the presence of sin in the world, "all creation has been groaning as in the pains of childbirth right up to the present time" (Romans 8:22). This world is still in Satan's grip, and that includes nature. Yet if we've learned anything in this study, it's that God is greater than any spiritual or natural force. God's irresistible will is that His saving message goes to the ends of the earth, and nothing can prevent that from happening. Though Satan's attacks may come our way and storms may rage around us, God is in control. Like Paul, we can trust Him to guide us as He uses us to accomplish His purposes, regardless of how rough the seas.

Sailing into a Storm (27:1-26)

October, A.D. 59—not a good time for a Mediterranean cruise. Some of the worst storms occur in this part of the world in the fall. We're about to see how bad they can get.

From Palestine to Crete (27:1-12)

From the change in the narrative, we can tell that Luke is a passenger on Paul's little cruise. Actually, it's not so little. This journey to Rome is going to eventually cover nearly 2000 miles. Joining Luke and Paul are Aristarchus, who was with Paul in Ephesus when the riot broke out (19:29), and a centurion by the name of Julius, who will show kindness to Paul (27:3) and will eventually save his life (27:42-43).

The first leg of their journey takes them north from Caesarea to Sidon, where Paul is allowed to visit friends. These are Christians Paul may have met previously on his trips to Jerusalem. We hope you've noticed throughout Acts how generous the believers in every city have been. Truly they are characterized by hospitality, love, and kindness, especially to one another. This is the way

Paul's Journey to Rome

the body of Christ should be. We all need the help and encouragement of others, and we all need to give others our help and our encouragement. Paul was the greatest and most courageous missionary in history, but he couldn't have accomplished what he did without a little help from his friends.

From Sidon the group sails to Myra in Lycia, where Julius books passage on an Egyptian vessel transporting grain to Rome. Passenger ships did not exist in the first century, so people commonly traveled by cargo ship.

From Myra the officers, crew, and prisoners—now numbering 276 people—sail south to Crete because the winds prevent them from going west. The ship ports at Fair Havens on the south side of Crete, where Paul warns the officers about the danger that lies ahead. There's no indication that this is a prophecy. The warning probably comes from Paul's extensive experience on the sea. Against Paul's advice, the centurion, the ship's captain, and the owner of the ship decide to sail for a better port. Big mistake.

A Change of Weather (27:13-26)

A wind of hurricane force comes up and drives the ship south. The crew takes several measures to save the ship, but nothing works. All hope is lost as the storm rages for several days. No doubt the men are seasick, hungry, and discouraged. That's when Paul stands up with a word of encouragement and a prophecy given to him by an angel. Because God wants Paul in Rome to stand trial before Caesar, He will preserve Paul and all who are with him. Paul gives credit to God, who is doing this out of His goodness.

> Times of trouble best discover the true worth of a man.
>
> —Thomas à Kempis

We can learn two lessons from this episode:

- *Great leaders always rise to the top in times of crisis.* Some leaders will take credit for their decisions, but leaders like Paul, whose strength is in the Lord, will always acknowledge their dependence on God.

- *As a Christian, you are a preservative.* Jesus has called us to be "salt of the earth" (Matthew 5:13). Salt is used for flavor, but it is also a preservative. Just as God used Paul to preserve the lives of those around him, God will use you to preserve people around you—if you are in the stream of His will and acknowledge Him as your source of strength.

Shipwrecked on Malta (27:27–28:10)

Two weeks have passed since the Egyptian ship sailed from Crete, pushed by the storms farther and farther west.

Abandon Ship! (27:27-38)

The sailors can't see a thing, but their depth soundings tell them they are getting close to land, so they drop anchor and wait for daybreak. Some of the crewmen try to abandon ship in the lifeboat, but Paul sees their ruse and alerts the centurion, who quickly cuts the ropes to the lifeboat. God's promise is that *everyone* would be saved (27:24). If some try to leave, all are in jeopardy. Let this be a lesson: Stick with the leader God has chosen.

Notice how Paul's influence continues to grow. He has been giving warnings, and now he is taking charge, encouraging the men to eat. Luke is encouraged by the fact that not one soul has been lost. That's the way it is in our Christian lives. We trust in the sovereignty of God, but we also exercise our judgment and act responsibly.

Paul's Life Is Spared (27:39-44)

When daybreak finally comes, the crew sees land and tries to steer the ship to the shore, but the ship hits a sandbar and the waves break her apart. Thinking the prisoners might escape, the soldiers want to kill them so their own lives won't be in jeopardy (remember the penalty for allowing prisoners to escape). But Julius, the centurion, wants to spare Paul. Once again, Paul is a preservative—this time for his fellow prisoners.

Miracles on Malta (28:1-10)

The islanders on Malta aren't Christians, but they are friendly and helpful. As Paul is helping to build a fire, a poisonous snake bites his hand, but it doesn't even faze him. Paul's prophecy that no one will lose their life extends to this tiny piece of real estate. The unplanned stopover on Malta turns into a mercy mission as Paul heals the father of Publius, the chief official of the island, as well as many other sick people. As a result, the people of Malta give Paul and the others honor and gifts. Such is often the case when God works wonders among people, even when they don't know God personally.

Rome At Last (28:11-31)

We're in the last section of Acts. In one sense, it's a bit anticlimactic. We don't know if Paul gets his day in the emperor's court. There's no big finish. The book just kind of trails off with Paul meeting friends and once again preaching to the Jewish leaders (notice that he never gives up on the Jews). Has Luke run out of steam, or is something else going on? We'll see in a minute.

A Welcome Sight (28:11-16)

After spending the winter on Malta, the beleaguered shipwreck survivors sail to Rome.

Actually, they sail to the port city of Puteoli, where they stay with some believers for a week. They still have to walk 130 miles up the Appian Way to Rome. The believers in Rome put out the welcome mat for Paul, renewing his courage. What sweet fellowship! Even though Paul is still a prisoner, he is given permission to rent a house and welcome visitors.

Paul Preaches (28:17-28)

Paul recounts his adventures to some Jewish leaders, telling them that he is a prisoner but innocent of any wrongdoing against the Jews (28:17). The Romans could find nothing to charge him with (28:18), but the Jewish leaders objected, forcing Paul to appeal to Caesar (28:19). Paul explains that he is being held because he believes that Jesus is the Messiah and hope of Israel (28:20).

Rome Is Just the Beginning

In this little sentence, "And so we came to Rome" (28:14), Luke opens all kinds of images. On one level, it marks the end of a remarkable journey that included imprisonment, death threats, royal court appearances, a harrowing sea journey, a shipwreck, and a snakebite. Truly Paul and all the believers associated with him understand the phrase, "God will make a way." On another level, Paul and Luke's arrival in this imperial city signals the beginning of a whole new chapter in the history of the church. From here the Gospel will spread across Europe and the Western world, penetrating new lands and people. The end of Acts is only the beginning.

These Roman Jews, unlike others Paul has encountered, have nothing against Paul. All they know is that "these Christians" are "denounced everywhere" (28:22). So Paul sets an information meeting at his house. He tells the large group about the Kingdom of God. The bottom line is that the Kingdom of God has come to them through the life, death, and resurrection of Jesus Christ. Some believe, and some leave, prompting Paul to deliver one more message. He quotes from Isaiah 6:9-10, which talks about the hardened hearts of God's people. They have shut out the very message and the very Savior that can give them forgiveness of sins, healing, and eternal life.

Is It All Over for Israel?

Paul is the first to acknowledge that this rejection of God's salvation by the Jews is not final. In his letter to the Romans, written several years earlier from Corinth, Paul wrote:

Did God's people stumble and fall beyond recovery? Of course not! His purpose was to make his salvation available to the Gentiles, and then the Jews would be jealous and want it for themselves. Now if the Gentiles were enriched because the Jews turned down God's offer of salvation, think how much greater a blessing the world will share when the Jews finally accept it (Romans 11:11-12).

Acts ends on a positive note as Paul continues to witness for Christ for two years under house arrest. Paul also writes his letters to the Ephesians, Colossians, and Philippians during this time. Truly the Gospel of Jesus Christ is going to the ends of the earth.

> *He welcomed all who visited him, proclaiming the Kingdom of God with all boldness and teaching about the Lord Jesus Christ. And no one tried to stop him* (Acts 30:31).

Epilogue

Luke doesn't tell us, but historians explain that Paul was released after two years and embarked on a fourth missionary journey, going as far as Spain (Romans 15:24,28). He wrote his first letter to Timothy and a letter to Titus during this time. He was again imprisoned in Rome, where he wrote his final letter (2 Timothy).

Knowing his life on earth was coming to an end, Paul wrote these immortal words:

> *I have fought a good fight, I have finished the race, and I have remained faithful. And now the prize awaits me—the crown of righteousness that the Lord, the righteous judge, will give me on the great day of his return. And the prize is not just for me but for all who eagerly look forward to his glorious return* (2 Timothy 4:7-8).

That's the challenge for us: to carry on the great commission of Jesus Christ, to fight the good fight, and to finish the race—all in the power of the Holy Spirit. That's why the story of Acts isn't really over. It continues in each of us as we look forward to the return of our Lord and Savior, Jesus Christ.

■ ■ ■

*S*tudy the *W*ord

1. Answer this question posed by William Larkin: "If the advance of the gospel is so unstoppable, what is stopping us from embracing it?"

2. When is the last time you weathered a storm? (We're using "storm" in the figurative sense. However, if you actually weathered a storm, you can talk about that too!) What did you learn that will help you next time your circumstances get difficult?

3. You may never be put into a position where you will literally preserve or save the life of another, but as a Christian, God has put you in a position where you can save the life of others spiritually. How might this change the way you see those who are lost?

4. At least twice during the journey to Rome, Paul, a veteran traveler, acted with common sense in order to help others in a time of crisis (see Acts 27:10,33-34). What experiences or skills do you have that could help others in a time of crisis?

5. What kind of regular fellowship are you involved in? This Bible study may be one way for you to meet with other believers. What else are you doing to enjoy the company of other Christians, and to contribute to their enjoyment and enrichment?

6. Explain what this statement means to you: "Pray as if it depends on God, and work as if it depends on you."

7. In what ways has the book of Acts impacted your life?

Appendix

A Chronology of Acts

Event	Date (A.D.)	Event	Date (A.D.)
The crucifixion, resurrection, and ascension of Jesus	30	Paul appears before Festus	59
The Day of Pentecost	30	Paul appears before Agrippa	59
The stoning of Stephen	33	Voyage to Rome	59–60
Paul's conversion	34	Philemon written	60
Paul's first missionary journey	47–48	Colossians written	60
Peter in Antioch	48–49	Ephesians written	60
Galatians written	49	Philippians written	61
The Jerusalem Council	49	Gospel of Luke written	61
Paul's second missionary journey	50–51	Acts written	62
1 and 2 Thessalonians written	50–51	Paul released from Roman house arrest	62
Paul's third missionary journey	52–56	Paul's possible trip to Spain	62
1 and 2 Corinthians written	54–55	1 Timothy written	62
Romans written	55	Titus written	63
Paul's arrest in Jerusalem	56	1 Peter written	63
Paul appears before Felix	57	Paul returns to Rome and is imprisoned	64
Paul's imprisonment in Caesarea	57	2 Timothy written	64
		Paul's death	64
		2 Peter written	64
		Peter's death	64
		Destruction of Jerusalem	70

Dig Deeper

*W*henever we write a book about God and His Word, we do a lot of research and reading. Here are the main books we used to write this Bible study on Acts. If you want to dig deeper into Acts and the Bible, here's a great place to start.

Commentaries

Acts by William J. Larkin Jr. is a scholarly and informative commentary. It offers deep theological insights.

One of our favorite New Testament Bible scholars is William Barclay. He's down to earth yet deep (a rare combination). We used his book *The Acts of the Apostles* from The New Daily Study Bible Series.

The Life Application Bible Commentary series is outstanding, and *Acts* was a big help. This commentary has plenty of what the title says—*application*.

The NIV Application Commentary on Acts by Ajith Fernando is excellent. We like the way he gives both the original meaning and the contemporary significance of each passage.

Pastor Kent Hughes offers a very practical view in *Acts: The Church Afire*. Each chapter contains several helpful illustrations drawn from contemporary life.

J. Vernon McGee is a favorite of many people because he is so down to earth. His two-volume commentary on Acts is very easy to follow.

If you want to know about the history and the culture of Bible times, you will love the *Zondervan Illustrated Bible Backgrounds Commentary*. The New Testament comes in four volumes. We used volume 2, which includes the excellent commentary on Acts by Clinton Arnold.

The New Testament volume of *The Bible Knowledge Commentary*, edited by John Walvoord and Roy Zuck, also provides valuable background and historical information. Stanley D. Toussaint wrote the chapter on Acts.

One of the best Bible commentary sets is the *Expositor's Bible Commentary*, edited by Frank R. Gaebelein. It's a bit more scholarly than the others, but sometimes you need a little more in-depth analysis. We used volume 9, which includes Acts by Richard N. Longenecker.

General Bible Study Helps

For general information about God and the Bible, check out our books, *Knowing God 101* and *Knowing the Bible 101*. They are written in the same user-friendly style as this book.

A Survey of the New Testament by Robert H. Gundry is our favorite New Testament survey book. Full of useful information, pictures, maps, and charts.

For dates and the chronology of the book of Acts, we relied on *Chronological and Background Charts of the New Testament* by H. Wayne House. The 75 charts in this excellent resource will help you keep the events of the New Testament in historical perspective.

For instruction and clarification on doctrinal issues, we use and recommend *Systematic Theology* by Wayne Grudem.

Bible Translations

Obviously you can't study Acts or the Bible without the primary source—the Bible! People often ask us, "Which Bible translation should I use?" We recommend that your primary study Bible be a *literal* translation (as opposed to a paraphrase), such as the *New International Version* (NIV) of the Bible or the *New American Standard Bible* (NASB). However, it's perfectly acceptable to use a Bible paraphrase, such as *The Living Bible* or *The Message* in your devotional reading.

Our personal choice is the *New Living Translation* (NLT), a Bible translation that uses a method called "dynamic equivalence." This means that the scholars who translated the Bible from the original languages (Hebrew and Greek) used a "thought-for-thought" translation philosophy rather than a "word-for-word" approach. It's just as accurate but easier to read. In the final analysis, the Bible that's best for you is the Bible you enjoy reading because you can understand it.

We used the NLT for just about all of our references in this Bible study. However, you will notice that we occasionally used the NIV and the NASB.

A Word About Personal Pronouns

When we write about God, we prefer to capitalize all personal pronouns that refer to God, Jesus, and the Holy Spirit. These would include *He, Him, His,* and *Himself.* However, not all writers follow this practice, and there's nothing wrong with that. In fact, personal pronouns for God were not capitalized in the original languages, which is why you'll find that the Bible uses *he, him, his,* and *himself.*

Bruce and Stan would enjoy hearing from you. Contact them with your questions, comments, or to schedule them to speak at an event.

Twelve Two Media
P.O. Box 25997
Fresno, CA 93729-5997

E-mail: info@twelvetwomedia.com

Web site: www.twelvetwomedia.com

Exclusive Online Feature

Here's a Bible study feature you're really going to like! Simply go online at:

www.christianity101online.com

There you'll find a Web site designed exclusively for users of the Christianity 101 Bible Studies series. When you log on to the site, just click on the book you are studying, and you will discover additional information, resources, and helps, including...

- *Background Material*—We can't put everything in this Bible study, so this online section includes more material, such as historical, geographical, theological, and biographical information.

- *More Questions*—Do you need more questions for your Bible study? Here are additional questions for each chapter. Bible study leaders will find this especially helpful.

- *Answers to Your Questions*—Do you have a question about something in your Bible study? Post your question and an "online scholar" will respond.

- *FAQ's*—In this section are answers to some of the more frequently asked questions about the book you are studying.

What are you waiting for? Go online and become a part of the Christianity 101 community!

Christianity 101® Bible Studies

Genesis: Discovering God's Answers to Life's Ultimate Questions

"In the beginning" says it all. Genesis sets the stage for the drama of human history. This guide gives you a good start and makes sure you don't get lost along the way.

John: Encountering Christ in a Life-Changing Way

This study reveals who Jesus is by demonstrating the dramatic changes He made in the lives of the people He met, including Nicodemus, the woman at the well, Lazarus, and John, "the disciple whom Jesus loved."

Acts: Living in the Power of the Holy Spirit

Bruce and Stan offer a straightforward look at the ongoing ministry of Jesus through the church. They highlight the drama of the early Christians' triumph over darkness and their explosive growth from a band of 120 fearful followers to a thriving, worldwide church.

Romans: Understanding God's Grace and Power

Paul's letter to the church in Rome is his clearest explanation and application of the good news. This fresh study of Romans assures you that the Gospel is God's answer to every human need.

1 & 2 Corinthians: Finding Your Unique Place in God's Plan

This enlightening study explores the apostle Paul's helpful responses to issues that churches continue to face today: maintaining unity in the church, exercising spiritual gifts, and identifying authentic Christian ministry.

Galatians: Walking in God's Grace

With their trademark humor, deep respect for the authority of Scripture, and penetrating insights into current trends, Bruce and Stan reveal the serious problems Paul addressed and practical solutions he provided. They show that his presentation of God's grace speaks as forcefully today as it did to his original readers.

Ephesians: Finding Your Identity in Christ

Verse for verse, the book of Ephesians is one of the most profound, powerful, and practical books in the Bible. This guide reveals the heart of Paul's teaching on who believers are in Christ.

Philippians/Colossians: Experiencing the Joy of Knowing Christ

This new 13-week study of two of Paul's most intimate letters will inspire you to know Christ more intimately and maintain your passion and vision. Filled with helpful background information, up-to-date applications, and penetrating, open-ended questions.

James: Working Out Your Faith

Bruce and Stan show that the New Testament book of James is bursting with no-nonsense help to help you grow in practical ways, such as perceiving God's will, maintaining a proper perspective on wealth and poverty, and demonstrating true wisdom in your speech and actions.

Revelation: Unlocking the Mysteries of the End Times

Have you ever read the final chapters of the Scriptures, only to finish with more questions than answers? Bruce and Stan help you understand Revelation's encouraging message and apply it to your life today.

Christianity 101® Studies

Now That You're a Christian

If you're a new believer, you'll connect with these honest, encouraging responses to questions that new Christians often have. You'll discover what God has done for humanity, how you can know Him better, and how you can reflect the love of Christ to people around you.

Bible Prophecy 101

In their contemporary, down-to-earth way, Bruce and Stan present the Bible's answers to your end-times questions. You will appreciate their helpful explanations of the rapture, the tribulation, the millennium, Christ's second coming, and other important topics.

Creation & Evolution 101

In their distinctive, easy-to-access style, Bruce and Stan explore the essentials of creation and evolution and offer fascinating evidence of God's hand at work. Perfect for individual or group use.

Knowing the Bible 101

Enrich your interaction with Scripture with this user-friendly guide, which shows you the Bible's story line and how each book fits into the whole. Learn about the Bible's themes, terms, and culture, and find out how you can apply the truths of every book of the Bible to your own life.

Knowing God 101

Whatever your background, you will be inspired by these helpful descriptions of God's nature, personality, and activities. You will also find straightforward responses to the essential questions about God.

Bible Answers 101

Using hundreds of questions from readers, Bruce and Stan tackle some of the biggest issues about life and living the Christian faith, including, *What happens when we die? Is Christ the only way to salvation? How can we know there is a God? Is the Bible true?*

Growing as a Christian 101

In this fresh look at the essentials of the Christian walk, Bruce and Stan offer you the encouragement you need to continue making steady progress in your spiritual life.

World Religions and Cults 101

This study features key teachings of each religion, quick-glance belief charts, biographies of leaders, and study questions. You will discover the characteristics of cults and how each religion compares to Christianity.

Evidence for Faith 101

Bruce and Stan present Christian apologetics without polemics and without clichés as they tackle vital questions people of all ages and beliefs are asking. Examine evidence—from history, from the lives of people changed by faith, and from our world—as you form and understand your convictions about God.